A Reference Guide to the

Royal Families

Families

What Every Reporter (or Royal Fan) Needs to Know

Table of Contents

Introduction

So you have been assigned to cover the latest royal wedding. That's easy enough: remark on the lovely flowers, oooh and aaah over the wedding dress, make fun of the more outlandish hats. Piece of cake, right?

Then you get there, and you see all of these very important looking people walking into the church. You have your royal expert on hand to point out the Prince of this and Duchess of that, and here you are, not even knowing where Liechtenstein is or why it has a Prince and not a King.

Don't want to feel stupid about royal families any more? This book is a basic guide to help reporters, and other royal watchers, identify European royalty of all stripes and give cursory information about who they are and why anyone cares.

This book will not make you an expert on Royalty. You still need your royal expert on hand to help with the finer points, but this guide can keep you from looking totally clueless.

First basic thing you need to know is that there is royalty outside of England! In fact, there are ten hereditary monarchies remaining in Europe. There are also a few dozen others spread around the globe, but this book is only focused on Europe. Of these ten monarchies, seven are kingdoms, two are principalities and one is a grand duchy.

What is the difference? Essentially, it comes down to what title the Head of State, or Sovereign, has. A Kingdom is ruled by a King or Queen, a Principality by a Prince or Princess, and a Grand Duchy by a Grand Duke or Grand Duchess. In the past, Europe also had Duchies (rules by Dukes) and Empires (ruled by Emperors). Germany had myriad other odd titles as well, but they all have been out of power for a century or more.

The second basic concept is there are titles and then there are "styles". A title is how a royal person is legally called in their country's laws. "Prince of the United Kingdom" is a title. Styles are what a particular royal should be called when talking about them specifically. "Prince Harry of Wales" is a style (his official title is Prince of the United Kingdom). Throughout this book, there will be examples where a person is titled one thing but called by a slightly different style, either out of convenience or tradition.

Thirdly, there is a difference between royalty and nobility. The quick and dirty way to explain the difference is that royalty reigns over a country, nobility does not. While there are nobles with the titles Duke, or even Prince, they are not Sovereign Dukes or Sovereign Princes. The man who rules Monaco is the (Sovereign) Prince of Monaco. However, there is also a Prince of Hohenlohe-Langenburg who rules over nothing, except his own household (and then only when his wife lets him). This book will talk about royalty, not nobility, except in cases when a noble person marries into a royal family, or a royal person is given an additional noble title.

Fourthly, the Royal Family is different than the family of the monarch. Each country has strict rules about who is considered a member of the Royal Family. However, the old saying "you can't pick your relatives" being true, there are going to be family members of the sovereign who are not members of the Royal Family. The differences will be made clear in each chapter.

Lastly, of the high-arching issues anyway, is the terminology. Sovereign and Reigning have very subtle differences, but we won't be going into that level of detail (that's what your royal expert is for). For our purposes, the words are pretty much interchangeable. Also interchangeable are the terms Monarch, Sovereign, or Head of State.

Another set of terms that tend to be misunderstood is Queen Mother versus Dowager Queen. To be styled as a Queen Mother, a lady had to have been Queen first (by right of being married to the late King) and be the mother of the current Sovereign. In Britain, the late Queen Mother who died in 2002 was the widow of King George VI and mother of Queen Elizabeth II so was entitled to the style Queen Mother. Assuming Prince Charles becomes King, his widow will be entitled to be styled The Queen while he lives. But after his death, she would not be the Queen Mother, because she is not the mother of the next King (presumedly the current Duke of Cambridge).

The term Dowager refers to the widow of a previous title holder, regardless of her relationship to the that person. If the married Duke of Somwhere dies and is succeeded by his bother, his widow is still the Dowager Duchess of Somewhere, and will remain so until her own death or she remarries. If there are widows of multiple Dukes of Somewhere still living at the same time, the widow of the first one to die retains the Dowager moniker, the rest being styled Firstname, Duchess of Somewhere.

Another term to know is "predicate," sometimes called a "qualification" in other texts. These are the phrases like "His Royal Highness" or "Her Majesty" that precede a title. Due to their length, we usually see them abbreviated. Below is a list of the abbreviations of predicates you will find in this book, from highest rank to the lowest:

H.M.	His or Her Majesty
H.I.H.	His or Her Imperial Highness
H.I. & R.H.	His or Her Imperial and Royal Highness
H.R.H	His or Her Royal Highness
H.H.	His or Her Highness
H.G.D.H.	His or Her Grand Ducal Highness
H.S.H.	His or Her Serene Highness

Each monarchy has its own rules governing the use of titles, and its own succession laws. These will be discussed in further detail in each chapter.

This book is divided by country. Each chapter will correspond to a current reigning monarchy, with the final chapter being a very quick overview of the former reigning royal families with highlights of what a reporter should know if one shows up at an event he or she is covering.

Each chapter (or country, if you like) will begin with the who, what, where, and when of the current monarch, followed by a discussion of their county's monarchy in a nutshell. This will be a very high overview of how the monarchy got to the point it is at today. Again, rely on your royal expert to fill in the details, that is what we get paid to do.

Next, there will be sections explaining the titles used by the family, and the laws of succession currently in force. One thing to keep in mind, the laws governing each of these have been in flux in most countries for the past decade or so, so be prepared for potential changes.

Once you have read enough to know the basics about the family, you will get a rundown of each of the active members of the Royal Family, with a picture to help you identify them. This is followed by a section of less detailed descriptions of the other family members you will need to know about to ably report on the event you are covering.

The final chapter, the one that covers the former royal families, is written to give you the most basic information of who is who among these families and what the likelihood is you may see them at your event.

Before I send you on you merry way, you need to know how to address royal people, as you may have the need to talk directly to them and "Hey, King!" just won't fly. There are just a few basic rules.

When referring to a member of the royal family in the 3rd person, it should be Her Majesty, His Royal Highness, etc. When reporting about the royal family, it is acceptable to use terms like "Prince Charles" or "Princess Kate," but be aware these terms are not technically correct. In longer discussions, such as newspaper or magazine articles, the correct title should be used early in the article and the more recognizable names may be used thereafter.

When meeting a member of any royal family in a social situation, you should not speak to them until they have spoken to you. In your first instance of addressing them, they should be called Your Royal Highness, Your Majesty, etc. and thereafter Sir or Ma'am. Ma'am should be said to rhyme with jam, not with bum (a common error made in movies). In a formal interview, it is acceptable for the interviewer to initiate the conversation.

Unless you are a subject of the royal you are meeting, you have no obligation to bow or curtsey to them. However, there is also nothing preventing you from doing so, except your own inability. In modern times, a gentleman's bow is made only with the head, not at the waist. A lady's curtsey has not changed since the middle ages and is something a lady has learned to do or she has not. If you have not been taught to curtsey properly, do not attempt it, you may hurt yourself or whomever you land on.

Finally, every January, a new edition of this book will be released, updated to be as current as possible. The goal will be to have it available in hard copy form as well as ebook form. If you find any information in here too complicated to understand, feel free to email me so I can try to explain it better in the next edition.

And if you are covering a royal event and are in need of a royal expert to help you, I am always available for that too.
Daniel Willis
Denver, Colorado, USA
daniel@dan-willis.com

Belgium

Current Sovereign: His Majesty King Albert II of the Belgians

Quick Life Facts:
Born: 6 Jun 1934, Stuyvenberg Castle, Brussels
Full names: Albert Felix Humbert Theodor Christian Eugène
    Marie
Father: H.M. Leopold III, King of the Belgians
Mother: H.R.H. Princess Astrid of Sweden and Norway
Married: 2 Jul 1959, Brussels
Wife: Donna Paolo Ruffo di Calabria
Ascended the Throne: 31 Jul 1993
Took Oath of Office: 9 Aug 1993
Children:
H.R.H. The Duke of Brabant (b.1960)
H.I. & R.H. Princess Astrid of Belgium, Archduchess of Austria-
    Este (b.1962)
H.R.H. Prince Laurent of Belgium (b.1963)
History of titles:
6 Jun 1934 - 31 Jul 1993: H.R.H. The Prince Liège

31 Jul 1993 - present: H.M. The King

The Belgian monarchy in a nutshell:
For centuries, Belgium was one of several provinces within the territory generally known as the Netherlands under the rule of, first Burgundy, then of the Habsburgs. Following the defeat of Napoleon in 1815, the Netherlands were made into an independent Kingdom under the House of Orange. In 1830, the Catholic portion successfully broke away to form the Belgian nation. In 1831, the Throne of the new country was offered to Prince Leopold of Saxe-Coburg and Gotha, the maternal uncle of Queen Victoria of Great Britain. Leopold was sworn in as King Leopold I.

Belgium has always been a divided country between two language groups. The northern half speak Flemish, a dialect of Dutch, and the south half speak Walloon, a dialect of French. The monarchy serves as a unifying force for these two halves. The capitol, Brussels, lies in the middle of the country and is officially bi-lingual. All signs, documents, etc. are produced in both languages.

King Leopold III, father of the current King, abdicated the Throne in 1951 and was succeeded by his eldest son, King Baudouin. While very popular with the people, Baudouin and his Queen, Fabiola, did not have any children, so the Throne passed to his brother upon his sudden death in 1993.

The Royal Family's Name
The house name of the royal family continues to be the House of Saxe-Coburg and Gotha. However, the royal family discontinued use of the Saxon titles during World War I. Technically, the Royal Family does not have a surname. If a need were to arise, a name would have to be created.

Titles within the Royal Family
Members of the Royal Family are titled His or Her Royal Highness Prince or Princess of Belgium. Various titles of nobility are available for the King to assign family members as he sees fit. The title Duke of Brabant is reserved for the heir-apparent, but is not an automatic title, it must be created in each instance. In 1991, the

succession laws were changed to allow female succession and to allow the first child to succeed regardless of gender. Princess Astrid then became 2nd in line to the Throne behind her elder (then unmarried) brother. The title Prince/Princess of Belgium was extended to her children in addition to the string of titles they possessed from their father, Archduke Lorenz of Austria-Este.

Ladies who marry into the family share their husband's title but retain their own given name. The exception is that the wife of the Duke of Brabant is not styled the Duchess of Brabant, but as Princess Mathilde.

Succession
Until 1991, the succession was limited to the male descendants of King Leopold I. Since 1991, the succession goes to the first-born regardless of gender. So an elder sister can succeed over a younger brother. Also, there is a marriage requirement. Any marriage within the family must have the consent of the Sovereign and be countersigned by a minister of state.
The Line of Succession:
1. H.R.H. The Duke of Brabant
2. H.R.H. Princess Elisabeth of Belgium
3. H.R.H. Prince Gabriel of Belgium
4. H.R.H. Prince Emanuel of Belgium
5. H.R.H. Princess Eléonore of Belgium
6. H.R.H. Princess Astrid of Belgium
7. H.I. & R.H. Prince Amadeo of Belgium
8. H.I. & R.H. Princess Maria Laura of Belgium
9. H.I. & R.H. Prince Joachim of Belgium
10. H.I. & R.H. Princess Luisa of Belgium
11. H.R.H Prince Laurent of Belgium
12. H.R.H. Princess Louise of Belgium
13. H.R.H. Prince Nicolas of Belgium
14. H.R.H. Prince Aymeric of Belgium

Members of the Royal Family

H.M. The Queen
Wife of the King
Born: 11 Sep 1937 Forte dei Marmi, Italy
Full names: Paola
Father: Prince Don Fulco Ruffo di
      Calabria, Duke of Guadia Lombarda
Mother: Countess Luisa Grazelli di
      Rossana e di Sebastiano
History of titles:
11 Sep 1937 - 2 Jul 1959: Donna Paola
Ruffo di Calabria
2 Jul 1959 - 31 Jul 1993: H.R.H. The Princess Liège
31 Jul 1993 - present: H.M. The Queen of the Belgians

H.M. Queen Fabiola of the Belgians
Sister-in-law of the King; widow of King
      Baudouin
Born: 11 Jun 1928 Madrid
Full names: Fabiola
Father: Don Gonzalo de Mora y Fernández,
      Marques de Casa Riera
Mother: Doña Blanca de Aragón y Carrillo
      de Albornoz
Married: 15 Dec 1960 Brussels
Husband: H.M. King Baudouin of the
      Belgians
No children
History of titles:
11 Jun 1928 - 15 Dec 1960: Doña Fabiola de Mora y de Aragón
15 Dec 1960 - 31 Jul 1993: H.M. The Queen of the Belgians
31 Jul 1993 - present: H.M. Queen Fabiola of Belgium

H.R.H. Prince Philippe, The Duke of Brabant
Son and heir-apparent of the King
Born: 15 Apr 1960 Belvédère Castle, near
    Laeken
Full names: Philipp Leopold Louis Marie
Father: H.M. The King of the Belgians
Mother: Donna Paola Ruffo di Calabria
Married: 4 Dec 1999 Brussels
Wife: Mathilde d'Udekem d'Acoz
Children:
H.R.H. Princess Elisabeth of Belgium (b.2001)
H.R.H. Prince Gabriel of Belgium (b.2003)
H.R.H. Prince Emmanuel of Belgium (b.2005)
H.R.H. Princess Eléonore of Belgium (b.2008)
History of titles:
15 Apr 1960 - 31 Jul 1993: H.R.H. Prince Philippe of Belgium
31 Jul 1993 - present: H.R.H. Prince Philippe, The Duke of
    Brabant

H.R.H. Princess Mathilde of Belgium
Daughter-in-law of the King
Born: 20 Jan 1973 Uccle, Belgium
Full names: Mathilde Marie Christiane
    Ghislaine
Father: Count Patrick d'Udekum d'Acoz
Mother: Countess Anna Maria Komorowska
History of titles:
20 Jan 1973 - 4 Dec 1999: Jonkvrouw
    Mathilde d'Udekum d'Acoz
4 Dec 1999 - present: H.R.H. Princess
    Mathilde of Belgium

Although married to the Duke of Brabant she does share this title.
At the time of her marriage she was created H.R.H. Princess
Mathilde of Belgium. Prior to her marriage, she carried the style
Jonkvrouw which indicated she was from a noble family but did
not have another title of her own.

H.R.H. Princess Elisabeth of Belgium
Granddaughter of the King
Born: 25 Oct 2001 Brussels
Full names: Elisabeth Thérèse Marie
Hélène
Father: H.R.H. The Duke of Brabant
Mother: Mathilde d'Udekeum d'Acoz

H.R.H. Princess Astrid of Belgium
Daughter of the King
Born: 5 Jun 1962 Belvédère Castle, near
	Laeken
Full names: Astrid Josephine-Charlotte
	Fabrizia Elizabeth Paola Marie
Father: H.M. The King of the Belgians
Mother: Donna Paola Ruffo di Calabria
Married: 22 Sep 1984 Brussels
Husband: H.I. & R.H. Archduke Lorenz of
Austria-Este
Children:
Prince Amadeo of Belgium (b.1986)
Princess Maria Laura of Belgium (b.1988)
Prince Joachim of Belgium (b.1991)
Princess Luisa of Belgium (b.1995)
Princess Laetitia of Belgium (b.2003)

Titles: In Belgium, Princess Astrid retains her title Princess of
Belgium only. According to her husband's family she would also
have the titles Archduchess of Austria-Este, Princess of Hungary
and Bohemia, Duchess of Modena. Her children are styled by the
Belgian title in Belgium. The Austrian Imperial Family would list
them by their father's titles first.

H.I. & R.H. Prince Lorenz of Belgium
Son-in-law of the King
Born: 16 Dec 1955 Boulogne-sur-Seine, France
Full names: Lorenz Otto Carl Amadeus Thadeus Maria Pius Andreas Marcus d'Aviano
Full titles: Archduke of Austria-Este, Prince of Hungary and Bohemia, Duke of Modena, Prince of Belgium
Father: H.I. & R.H. Archduke Robert of Austria-Este, Duke of Modena
Mother: H.R.H. Princess Margherita of Savoy
History of titles:
19 Dec 1955 - 11 Oct 1995: H.I. & R.H. Archduke Lorenz of Austria-Este, Prince of Hungary and Bohemia, Prince of Modena
11 Oct 1995 - 7 Feb 1996: H.I. & R.H. Archduke Lorenz of Austria-Este, Prince of Hungary and Bohemia, Prince of Modena, Prince of Belgium
7 Feb 1996 - present: H.I. & R.H. Archduke Lorenz of Austria-Este, Prince of Hungary and Bohemia, Prince of Belgium, The Duke of Modena

Lorenz's father was the 2nd son of Austria Emperor Karl I and as such became the heir to the Duchy of Modena, then incorporated into the Kingdom of Italy. Upon his death in 1996, Lorenz became the claimant to that Duchy. This is also why Este is added to the end of Austria.

In Belgium, Lorenz is styled as H.R.H. Prince Lorenz of Belgium followed by the rest of the titles. In his own family he is styled by the Austrian titles first with H.I. & R.H. (His Imperial and Royal Highness). His children have the same dual styling depending on which family you ask.

H.R.H. Prince Laurent of Belgium

Son of the King
Born: 19 Oct 1963 Belvédère Castle, near
    Laeken
Full names: Laurent Benoit Baudouin
    Marie
Father: H.M. The King of the Belgians
Mother: Donna Paola Ruffo di Calabria
Married: 12 Apr 2003 Brussels
Wife: Claire Coombs
Children:
H.R.H. Princess Louise of Belgium
    (b.2004)
H.R.H. Prince Nicolas of Belgium (b.2005) (twin)
H.R.H. Prince Aymeric of Belgium (b.2005) (twin)

H.R.H. Princess Claire of Belgium

Daughter-in-law of the King
Born: 18 Jan 1974 Bath, England
Full names: Claire Louise
Father: Nicholas Coombs
Mother: Nicole Mertens
History of titles:
18 Jan 1974 - 12 Apr 2003: Miss Claire
    Coombs
12 Apr 2003 - present: H.R.H. Princess
    Claire of Belgium

Other Family Members

Delphine Boël Illegitimate daughter of the King. Her mother is
Sybille, Baroness de Selys Longchamps who was married to
Jacques Boël at the time of Delphine's birth. King Albert has not
publicly acknowledged his daughter, but is said to have done so
privately. For their part, neither Sybille nor Delphine have
commented on her paternity. Delphine is now the mother of
Josephine and Oscar O'Hare by her companion, James O'Hare.

H.R.H. Princess Marie-Christine of Belgium (b.1951) Half-sister of the King, daughter of King Leopold III and his 2nd wife, Lillian Baels, who was styled Princess de Rethy after the marriage. The children of this 2nd marriage do not have succession rights and are not considered part of the Royal Family. A controversial figure, she lives in the U.S. with her 2nd husband Jean-Paul Gourges and has no children

H.R.H. Princess Marie-Esmerelda of Belgium (b.1956) Half-sister of the King, daughter of Leopold III and his 2nd wife, the Princess de Rethy. In Britain, Marie-Esmerelda may also be styled as Lady Moncada as she is married to Sir Salvador Moncada. They have two children, **Alexandra Moncada** (b.1998) and **Leopoldo Moncada** (b.2001). Professionally, she is a journalist writing under the name Esmerelda de Rethy

H.R.H. Princess Alexandre of Belgium (b.1951) Sister-in-law of the King, widow of Prince Alexandre (1942-2009), the King's half-brother. She was born Léa Wolman and had been married twice before marrying Prince Alexandre. She has one child be each of those marriages, but none by Alexandre. Alexandre married without asking for the King's consent and he is not a member of the Royal Family so his wife is styled as Princess Alexandre rather than Princess Léa

H.R.H. Grand Duke Jean of Luxembourg (b.1921) Brother-in-law of the King, widower of Grand Duchess Josephine-Charlotte who was born a Princess of Belgium. For information on this family see the article on Luxembourg.

Photo Acknowledgements:
All photos in this section are courtesy of *The Belgian Royal House.*

Denmark

Current Sovereign: Her Majesty Queen Margrethe II of Denmark

Quick Life Facts:
Born: 16 Apr 1940 Amalienborg Palace, Copenhagen
Full names: Margrethe Alexandrine Thorhildur Ingrid
Full titles: Queen of Denmark (all other traditional titles were
    abandoned upon her ascension)
Father: H.M. King Frederik IX of Denmark
Mother: H.R.H. Princess Ingrid of Sweden
Married: 10 Jun 1967 Copenhagen
Husband: Henri de Laborde de Monpezat (H.R.H. Prince Henrik)
Ascended the Throne: 14 Jan 1972
Children:
H.R.H. Crown Prince Frederik of Denmark (b.1968)
H.R.H. Prince Joachim of Denmark (b.1969)
History of titles:
16 Apr 1940 - 14 Jan 1972
14 Jan 1972 - present: H.M. The Queen of Denmark

Danish monarchy in a nutshell:
Ancient Danish history is lost in the murkiness of the Viking sagas,
but the Royal Family is generally reckoned to have started with

King Gorm who reigned in the early 900's. The House of Oldenburg, the male line ancestors of the present Royal Family came to the Throne in 1448 with the election of Christian I, a descendant through female lines of the house of Gorm. With the sole exception of Christian I's son, every King since 1448 has alternated between the names Christian and Frederik until the present Queen ascended in 1972.

The Throne was elective until 1661, but in practice, the next male in the House of Oldenburg was always elected as the next king. These elections took place during the lifetime of the previous king so there would be no period of confusion between reigns. In 1661, the Throne was declared hereditary following the principles of Salic Law which forbade women from succeeding.

In 1863, the senior line of the Oldenburgs became extinct in the male line with the death of King Frederik VII. During Frederik's last few years, the Danish Parliament agreed to elect a younger son from the junior most line of the house of Oldenburg, Prince Christian of Schleswig-Holstein-Sonderburg-Glücksburg as the heir to the Throne. It is this mouthful that is the Royal House of Denmark to this day.

Prince Christian, who reigned as Christian IX, is called the "Grandfather of Europe" because his eldest son ruled Denmark, his second son was elected to the Throne of Greece, the eldest daughter married Edward VII of Great Britain and the second daughter married Emperor Alexander III of Russia. Additionally, one grandson was elected to the newly independent Throne of Norway, and another married the sister of the German Kaiser.

The extended Royal Family today is made up of the male line descendants of Christian IX. By 1953, it had become clear that the then King and Queen, Frederik IX and Queen Ingrid, were not going to have any more children than the three daughters they already had. Parliament changed the succession laws to allow for female succession leading to the ascension of Margrethe II in 1972.

Name of Royal Family:

The members of the royal family have no surname. They belong to the House of Schleswig-Holstein-Sonderburg-Glücksburg which also includes the ducal house of that name, and the royal families of Greece, and Norway.

Titles of the Royal Family:
Members of the Royal Family are titled Prince or Princess of Denmark. The children of the Sovereign and the children of the heir-apparent have the predicate His or Her Royal Highness. Other family members have the predicate His or Her Highness. Ladies who marry into the family are traditionally styled by their own first name so the wife of Prince Joachim is not Princess Joachim, but Princess Marie.

When a member of the Royal Family marries without the consent of the Sovereign, they cease to be a member of the Royal Family and are stripped of their royal titles. Traditionally, the sovereign has created the title Count af Rosenborg for these former Princes.

The heir-apparent carries the title Crown Prince. Also, the children and grandchildren of Queen Margrethe are additionally titled Count or Countess de Monpezat since 30 Apr 2008.

Succession:
The Constitution of 1661 provided for male-only primogeniture succession. In 1953, the Constitution was amended to allow female succession but to still give male preference among siblings, and also limited the succession to the descendants of King Christian X. In 2009, the Constitution was further amended to remove the male preference. Additional decrees from King Frederik IX bar his youngest daughter, Queen Anne Marie and her descendants from the line of succession because she is married to a foreign Sovereign. He also decreed his middle daughter Princess Benedikte would remain in the line of succession but her children would not unless they were raised in Denmark (which they weren't).
Line of Succession:
1. H.R.H. Crown Prince Frederik of Denmark
2. H.R.H. Prince Christian of Denmark
3. H.R.H. Princess Isabella of Denmark

4. H.R.H. Prince Vincent of Denmark
5. H.R.H. Princess Josephine of Denmark
6. H.R.H. Prince Joachim of Denmark
7. H.H. Prince Nikolai of Denmark
8. H.H. Prince Felix of Denmark
9. H.H. Prince Henrik of Denmark
10. H.R.H. The Princess of Sayn-Wittgenstein-Berleberg
11. H.H. Princess Elisabeth of Denmark

Members of the Royal Family

H.R.H. Prince Henrik, Prince Consort of Denmark
Husband of the Queen
Born: 11 Jun 1934 Talance, France
Full names: Henri Marie Jean André
Father: Count André de Laborde de Monpezat
Mother: Renée Doursenot
Married: 10 Jun 1967 Copenhagen
History of titles:
11 Jun 1934 - 10 Jun 1967: Henri de Laborde de Monpezat
10 Jun 1967 - 14 Jan 1972: H.R.H. Prince Henrik of Denmark
14 Jan 1972 - present: H.R.H. Prince Henrik, Prince Consort of Denmark

H.R.H. Crown Prince Frederik of Denmark
Son and heir-apparent of the Queen
Born: 26 May 1968 Copenhagen
Full names: Frederik André Henrik Christian
Full titles: Crown Prince of Denmark, Count af Monpezat
Father: H.R.H. Prince Henrik, Prince Consort of Denmark
Mother: H.M. the Queen of Denmark
Married: 14 May 2004 Copenhagen
Wife: Mary Donaldson
Children:

24

H.R.H. Prince Christian of Denmark (b.2005)
H.R.H. Princess Isabella of Denmark (b.2007)
H.R.H. Prince Vincent of Denmark (b.2011) (twin)
H.R.H. Princess Josephine of Denmark (b.2011) (twin)
History of titles:
26 May 1968 - 14 Jan 1972: H.R.H. Prince Frederik of Denmark
14 Jan 1972 - present: H.R.H. Crown Prince Frederik of Denmark

H.R.H. Crown Princess Mary of Denmark
Daughter-in-law of the Queen
Born: 5 Feb 1972 Hobart, Tasmania
Full names: Mary Elizabeth
Full titles: Crown Princess of Denmark,
    Countess af Monpezat
Father: John Donaldson
Mother: Henrietta (Etta) Home
History of titles:
5 Feb 1972 - 14 May 2004: Miss Mary
Donaldson
14 May 2004 - present: H.R.H. Crown Princess Mary of Denmark

H.R.H. Prince Christian of Denmark
Grandson of the Queen
Born: 15 Oct 2005 Capenhagen
Full names: Christian Vlademr Henri John
Full titles: Prince of Denmark
Father: H.R.H. Crown Prince Frederik of
Denmark
Mother: Mary Donaldson
History of titles:
15 Oct 2005 - present: H.R.H. Prince Christian
of Denmark

H.R.H. Prince Joachim of Denmark
Son of the Queen
Born: 7 Jun 1969 Copenhagen
Full names: Joachim Holger Valdemar
    Christian
Full titles: Prince of Denmark, Count af
    Monpezat
Father: H.R.H. Prince Henrik, Prince Consort
    of Denmark
Mother: H.M. the Queen of Denmark
Married (1) 18 Nov 1995 Hillerød (divorced
2005)
First wife: Alexandra Manley
Married (2) 24 May 2008 Copenhagen
Second wife: Marie Cavallier
Children:
by 1st marriage:
H.H. Prince Nikolai of Denmark (b.1999)
H.H. Prince Felix of Denmark (b.2002)
by 2nd marriage:
H.H. Prince Henrik of Denmark (b.2009)
a fourth child is due in late January 2012

H.R.H. Princess Marie of Denmark
Daughter-in-law of the Queen
Born: 7 Jun 1969 Paris
Full names: Marie Agathe Odile
Full titles: Princess of Denmark, Countess af
    Monpezat
Father: Alain Cavallier
Mother: François Grassiot
History of titles:
7 Jun 1969 - 24 May 2008: Mademoiselle Marie Cavallier
24 May 2008 - present: H.R.H. Princess Marie of Denmark

H.R.H. Princess Benedikte, Princess of Sayn-Wittgenstein-Berleberg
Sister of the Queen
Born: 29 Apr 1944 Amalienborg Palace
Full names: Benedikte Astrid Ingeborg Ingrid
Full titles: Princess of Denmark, Princess of
    Sayn-Wittgenstein-Berleberg
Father: H.M. King Frederik IX of Denmark
Mother: H.R.H. Princess Ingrid of Sweden
Married: 3 Feb 1968 Fredenborg Palace, Denmark
Husband: H.H. Richard, Prince of Sayn-Wittgenstein-Berleberg
Children:
H.H. Hereditary Prince Gustav of Sayn-Wittgenstein-Berleberg
    (b.1969)
H.H. Countess Alexandra von Pfeil und Klein-Ellguth (b.1970)
H.H. Princess Nathalie, Frau Johannsmann (b.1975)
History of titles:
39 Apr 1944 - 3 Feb 1968: H.R.H. Princess Benedikte of Denmark
3 Feb 1968 - present: H.R.H. Princess Benedikte, Princess of Sayn-
    Wittgenstein-Berleberg

H.H. The Prince of Sayn-Wittgenstein-Berleberg
Brother-in-law to the Queen
Born: 29 Jul 1934 Giessen, Germany
Full names: Richard-Casimir Karl August
    Robert Konstantin
Father: H.S.H. Gustav Albrecht, Prince of Sayn-
Wittgenstein-
    Berleberg
Mother: Marguerite Fouché d'Otrante
History of titles:
29 Jul 1934 - 3 Feb 1968: H.S.H. Hereditary Prince Richard of
    Sayn-Wittgenstein-Berleberg
3 Feb 1968 - 29 Nov 1969: H.H. Hereditary Prince Richard of
    Sayn-Wittgenstein-Berleberg
29 Nov 1969 - present: H.H. The Prince of Sayn-Wittgenstein-
    Berleberg

Prince Richard's father went missing in action in Russia in 1944 but was not declared dead until 1969. Upon his marriage, his father-in-law granted him the predicate Highness, having previously been His Serene Highness (Sein Durchlaucht in German). This was also extended to his children.

H.H. Princess Elisabeth of Denmark
1st cousin of the Queen
Born: 8 May 1935 Copenhagen
Full names: Elisabeth Caroline-Mathilde
    Alexandrine Helena Olga Thyra Feodora
    Estrid Margrethe Désirée
Father: H.R.H. Prince Knud of Denmark
Mother: H.H. Princess Caroline Mathilde of Denmark
unmarried

Elisabeth's parents were first cousins to one another. Her father was a son of King Christian X. Her mother was a granddaughter of King Frederik VIII and daughter of Prince Harald.

Other Family Members

H.M. Queen Anne-Marie of the Hellenes (b.1946) Youngest sister of the Queen. She is married to **King Constantine II**. Often called the King and Queen of Greece, this title is not correct. The correct title King and Queen of the Hellenes. Other members of that family are Princes or Princesses of Greece. All members of the Greek Royal Family are descended in the male line from King Christian IX of Denmark so are also titled Prince or Princess of Denmark. King Constantine and Queen Anne-Marie have two unmarried children: **Princess Theodora of Greece** (b.1983) and **Prince Philippos of Greece** (*1986). Their married children are listed next.

H.R.H. Crown Prince Pavlos of Greece (b.1967) Nephew of the Queen, son of Queen Anne-Marie of the Hellenes. He is married to Marie-Chantal Miller, now Crown Princess Marie. They have five children: **Princess Maria-Olympia** (b.1996), **Prince Constantine-Alexios** (b.1998), **Prince Achilles-Andreas** (b.2000), **Prince Odysseus Kimon** (b.2004), and **Prince Aristidis-Stavros** (b.2008)

H.R.H. Princess Alexia of Greece, Señora Morales (b.1965) Niece of the Queen, daughter of Queen Anne-Marie of the Hellenes. She is married since 1999 to Carlos Morales y Quintana. They have four children all surnamed Morales y de Grecia: **Arrietta** (b.2002), **Ana-Maria** (b.2003), **Carlos** (b.2005), and **Amelia** (b.2007)

H.R.H. Prince Nikolaos of Greece (b.1969) Nephew of the Queen, daughter of Queen Anne-Marie of the Hellenes. He married Tatiana Blatnik in 2010. They are expecting their first child in the spring of 2012.

H.H. Hereditary Prince Gustav of Sayn-Wittgenstein-Berleberg (b.1969) Nephew of the Queen, son of Princess Benedikte. He has taken over the duties of his father including the running of the Castle Berleberg since 2003. He is unmarried.

H.H. Countess Alexandra von Pfeil und Klein-Ellguth (b.1970) Niece of the Queen, daughter of Princess Benedikte. Née Princess of Sayn-Wittgenstein-Berleberg, she married in 1998 to **Count Jefferson von Pfeil und Klein-Ellguth** and they have two children: **Count Richard** (b.1999) and **Countess Ingrid** (b.2003)

H.H. Nathalie Johannsmann (b.1975) Niece of the Queen, daughter of Princess Benedikte. Née Princess of Sayn-Wittgenstein-Berleberg, she married in 2010 to **Alexander Johannsmann** and has one child: **Konstantin** (b.2010)

Countess Alexandra af Rosenborg (b.1964) former daughter-in-law of the Queen, ex-wife of Prince Joachim. Née Alexandra Manley, after her divorce she was allowed to keep the title H.R.H. Princess of Denmark and was created the additional title Countess af Rosenborg. She remarried in 2007 to Martin Jørgensen losing the title H.R.H. Princess but retaining Countess af Rosenborg. She is the mother of Prince Joachim's eldest two children, but has not had any children with her second husband.

Photo Credits:
All photos in this section are from the author's collection.

Great Britain

Current Sovereign: Her Majesty Queen Elizabeth II of the United Kingdom of Great Britain and Northern Ireland.

Quick Life facts:
Born: 21 Apr 1926 in Mayfair, London
Full Name: Elizabeth Alexandra Mary
Full Titles: Her Majesty, Elizabeth the Second, By the Grace of
    God, of the United Kingdom of Great Britain and Northern
    Ireland, and Her Dominions beyond the Seas, Queen, Head of
    the Commonwealth, Defender of the Faith
Father: King George VI
Mother: Lady Elizabeth Bowes-Lyons (later the Queen Mother)
Married: 20 Nov 1947 Westminster Abbey, London
Husband: H.R.H. The Duke of Edinburgh (né Prince of Greece)
Ascended the Throne: 6 Feb 1952
Crowned: 2 Jun 1952 in Westminster Abbey (Britain is the only
country to have a coronation ceremony, most others have a
swearing in)
Children:

H.R.H The Prince of Wales (b.1948)
H.R.H. The Princess Royal (b.1950)
H.R.H. The Duke of York (b.1960)
H.R.H. The Earl of Wessex (b.1964)
History of Titles:
21 Apr 1926 - 10 Dec 1936: H.R.H. Princess Elizabeth of York
10 Dec 1936 - 20 Nov 1947: H.R.H. The Princess Elizabeth
20 Nov 1947 - 6 Feb 1952: H.R.H. The Duchess of Edinburgh
6 Feb 1952 - present: H.M. The Queen

The British monarchy in a nutshell:
The Royal Family of Great Britain, is really the joining of the
Royal Families of England and Scotland, two separate kingdoms
with two separate royal families until 1603 when King James VI of
Scotland succeeded Queen Elizabeth I of England, joining the two
countries under one crown. The union was formalized in 1707 with
founding the of the Kingdom of Great Britain. In 1814, the name
of the country was changed again to the United Kingdom of Great
Britain and Ireland, that last piece being changed to Northern
Ireland after the Republic of Ireland was created in 1922.

The beginning of the English Royal Family is reckoned with the
Norman Invasion of 1066. William of Normandy became King
William I and every King (or Queen) of England, Great Britain,
and the United Kingdom has been descended from him. In
Scotland, the oldest provable King was Kenneth I who died in 858.
All subsequent Kings of Scotland were descended from him.

Today the British monarchy is thought of in terms of the
descendants of King George V (d.1936), the current Sovereign
being his granddaughter, Queen Elizabeth II.

The Royal Family's Name: First it must be understood there is a
difference between the family surname and the name of the House.
The name of the House has been Windsor since 1917 when the
Germanic name Saxe-Coburg and Gotha was dropped because of
anti-German feelings in World War I. Windsor was selected
because it was inherently English and because Windsor Castle has
been a royal residence for centuries.

In 1960, the Queen decreed that while the House name would remain Windsor for future generations, the surname of her children and male-line descendants would be Mountbatten-Windsor in acknowledgement of her husband's surname, Mountbatten.

Titles in the Royal Family: The Sovereign is titled the King or the Queen. The wife a King is also titled Queen. Kings and Queens enjoy the predicate His/Her Majesty. If the Sovereign is female, her husband does not automatically get the title of King. However, she has the right to create the title for him, but no Queen has done this since Queen Mary I in the 1500's.

The only other royal title in Britain is Prince or Princess with the predicate His/Her Royal Highness. In 1917, King George V issued a decree (called a Letters Patent) that limited the royal title to only the children of a Sovereign, the children of the sons of a Sovereign, and the eldest son of the eldest son of the heir-apparent. Wives of princes share their husbands' titles, but husbands of princesses do not. When a non-royal lady marries into the British royal family she does not become Princess her-first-name, she shares whatever title her husband has. When the Duke of York married, his wife was the Duchess of York, not Princess Sarah and not Duchess Sarah. When Prince Michael of Kent married, his wife became Princess Michael of Kent, not Princess Marie-Christine. This a titling system unique to Britain. In other European counties, ladies would keep their own first name.

All princes and princesses are Prince or Princess of the United Kingdom if they are descended from King George VI (Elizabeth II's father). Those descended from other sons of King George V continue to be titled with the older form: Prince/Princess of Great Britain and Ireland. However, they are rarely *styled* either way. The children of the monarch are simply styled Prince/Princess Firstname with the article 'The' in front of their name, such as The Prince Andrew, etc. Grandchildren of the Sovereign loose the "The" and are styled according to their father's noble title. For example, the daughter of the Duke of Kent is styled Princess

Alexandra of Kent, although this does changes the fact that she is titled as a Princess of Great Britain and Ireland.

Descendants of British monarchs in the male line who are too distantly related to be titled Prince/Princess are commoners. The first generation of such commoners are styled Lord or Lady Firstname Windsor (or Mountbatten-Windsor for descendants of Elizabeth II). After that generation, they are simply Mr. or Miss.

It is traditional for the sons of the monarch to receive additional noble titles when they marry. (The Prince of Wales is a special case and will be discussed under his own entry.) Traditionally this added title is a Dukedom and has secondary titles such as an Earldom, a Viscountcy and/or a Barony with it. Prince Edward was an exception, see his entry for details. The title is typically created just prior to the wedding so when the marriage happens, the bride will immediately be the Duchess of X rather than Princess husband's-firstname.

Succession:
The British succession laws are spelled out in the Act of Settlement (1701) which limits the succession to the non-Catholic descendants of Electress Sophia of Hanover (1640-1714), mother of King George I. Not only can no Catholic ascend the Throne, but no one who married a Catholic can either. However, if a person marries a Catholic but raises their children as non-Catholics, those children would remain in succession. Another document worth mentioning is the Royal Marriages Act (1772) which invalidates any marriage of a member of the royal family if it does not have the consent of the Sovereign. This latter law has not been an issue since the early 1800's.

The succession follows the rules of male-preference primogeniture, which means women can succeed if they have no surviving brother or brother's issue. The current Queen became queen because she had no brothers and she was the elder of her father's two daughters. The succession goes to the eldest son, or to his eldest son if he is already deceased. If the eldest son is deceased with no heirs, it goes to the next son. After children of the Sovereign his/her siblings and their descendants would be next following the same rules, then uncles, cousins, and so on.

In the fall of 2011, Parliament began the process for the changing the succession laws to remove the male preference and allow descendants to marry Roman Catholics and allow at least certain desendants to marry without the Sovereigns permission. These changes, when enacted, are expected to affect only the descendants of the Duke of Cambridge and not be retro-active to other family members, but that will depend on the laguage of the law that does eventually gets passed.

The current number of people with theoretical places in line to the Throne is quite extensive. It is approximately 5000 people long accounting for all non-Catholic legitimate descendants of Electress Sophia. The list below is the top 10 and does not take into account any changes that Parliament is still considering but has not yet acted upon.

The Line of Succession:
1. H.R.H. The Prince of Wales
2. H.R.H. The Duke of Cambridge
3. H.R.H. Prince Harry of Wales
4. H.R.H. The Duke of York
5. H.R.H. Princess Beatrice of York
6. H.R.H. Princess Eugenie of York
7. H.R.H. The Earl of Essex
8. Viscount Severn
9. Lady Louise Mountbatten-Windsor
10. H.R.H. The Princess Royal

Members of the Royal Family

H.R.H. The Duke of Edinburgh
Husband to the Queen
Born: 10 Jun 1921 in Corfu, Greece
Full names: Philip
Full titles: Prince of the United Kingdom,
 Duke of Edinburgh, Earl of Merioneth,
 Baron Greenwich
Father: H.R.H. Prince Andrew of Greece
Mother: H.S.H. Princess Alice of
Battenberg
Married: 20 Nov 1947, Westminster
 Abbey
Wife: H.M. The Queen

History of titles:
10 Jun 1921 - 10 Mar 1947: H.R.H Prince Philip of Greece and
 Denmark
10 Mar 1947 - 20 Nov 1947: Lt. Philip Mountbatten
20 Nov 1947 - 22 Feb 1957: H.R.H. The Duke of Edinburgh
22 Feb 1957 - present: H.R.H. The Prince Philip, The Duke of
 Edinburgh

Prince Philip of Greece renounced his Greek titles after asking for
Elizabeth's hand in marriage. On his wedding day, his father-in-
law, King George VI, created the title Duke of Edinburgh with the
predicate His Royal Highness. It seemed to have been overlooked
that he was not a prince at that point. His wife corrected that in
1957 by creating him a Prince of the United Kingdom

H.R.H. The Prince of Wales
Son and heir-apparent to the Queen
Born: 14 Nov 1948 at Buckingham Palace
Full name: Charles Philip Arthur George
Full titles: Prince of the United Kingdom,
    Prince of Wales and Earl of Chester,
    Duke of Cornwall, Duke of Rothesay,
    Earl of Carrick, Baron Renfrew, Lord of
    the Isles and Great Stewart of Scotland
Father: H.R.H. The Duke of Edinburgh
Mother: H.M. The Queen
Married (1): 29 Jul 1981, St. Paul's Cathedral (divorced 1996)
First wife: Lady Diana Spencer (d.1997)
Married (2): 9 Nov 2005, Windsor (civil only)
Second wife: Mrs. Camilla Parker Bowles (née Shand)
Children (of 1st marriage):
H.R.H. The Duke of Cambridge (b.1982)
H.R.H. Prince Harry of Wales (b.1984)
History of Titles:
14 Nov 1948 - 6 Feb 1952: H.R.H. Prince Charles of Edinburgh
6 Feb 1952 - 26 Jul 1958: H.R.H. The Duke of Cornwall
26 Feb 1958 - present: H.R.H. The Prince of Wales

The titles Prince of Wales and Earl of Chester are reserved exclusively for the son of the Sovereign. He does not get them automatically, they have to be created for him. The remainder of his titles, Duke of Cornwall, etc. are automatic and he succeeds to these titles when his parent ascends the Throne. Should he die prior to becoming King, his son will not inherit his titles as they are exclusive to the eldest son. If a Prince of Wales dies without issue, the title can be recreated for his next younger brother who will then be the eldest surviving son of the Sovereign.

H.R.H. The Duchess of Cornwall
Daughter-in-Law of the Queen
Born: 17 Nov 1947 London
Full names: Camilla Rosemary
Father: Bruce Shand
Mother: The Hon. Rosalind Cubitt
Married (1): 4 Jul 1973(divorced 1995)
First husband: Andrew Parker Bowles
Children (of 1st marriage):
Tom Parker Bowles (b.1974)
Mrs. Harry (Laura) Lopes (b.1978)
History of titles:
17 Nov 1947 - 4 Jul 1973: Miss Camilla Shand
4 Jul 1973 - 3 Mar 1995: Mrs. Andrew Parker Bowles
3 Mar 1995 - 9 Nov 2005: Mrs. Camilla Parker Bowles
9 Nov 2005 - present: H.R.H. The Duchess of Cornwall

Though styled as the Duchess of Cornwall, she is also legally titled Princess of Wales and all of the other titles of her husband. The decision was made to be styled as such out of courtesy to the public sentiment towards Diana, Princess of Wales.

H.R.H. The Duke of Cambridge
Grandson of the Queen
Born: 21 Jun 1982 St. Mary's Hospital,
    Paddington
Full names: William Arthur Philip Louis
Full titles: Prince of the United Kingdom,
    Duke of Cambridge, Earl of Strathearn,
    Baron Carrickfergus
Father: H.R.H. The Prince of Wales
Mother: Lady Diana Spencer
Married: 29 Apr 2011 Westminster Abbey
Wife: Catherine Middleton
History of titles:
21 Jun 1982 - 29 Apr 2011: H.R.H. Prince William of Wales
29 Apr 2011 - present: H.R.H. The Duke of Cambridge

H.R.H. The Duchess of Cambridge
Granddaughter-in-Law of Queen
Born: 9 Jan 1982 Reading, Berkshire
Full names: Catherine Elizabeth
Father: Michael Middleton
Mother: Carole Goldsmith
Married: 29 Apr 2011 Westminster Abbey
Husband: H.R.H. The Duke of Cambridge
History of titles:
9 Jan 1982 - 29 Apr 2011: Miss Catherine
    "Kate" Middleton
29 Apr 2011 - present: H.R.H. The Duchess of Cambridge

H.R.H. Prince Harry of Wales
Grandson of the Queen
Born: 15 Sep 1984, St. Mary's Hospital,
    Paddington
Full names: Henry Charles Albert David
Father: H.R.H. The Prince of Wales
Mother: Lady Diana Spencer

Although formally christened Henry, he has
always been styled as Prince Harry.

H.R.H. The Duke of York
Son of the Queen
Born: 19 Feb 1960, Buckingham Palace
Full names: Andrew Albert Christian
    Edward
Full titles: Prince of the United Kingdom,
    Duke of York, Earl of Inverness, Baron
    Killyleagh
Father: H.R.H. The Duke of Edinburgh
Mother: H.M. The Queen
Married: 23 Jul 1986, Westminster Abbey (divorced 1986)
Former wife: Sarah, Duchess of York (née Ferguson)
Children:
H.R.H. Princess Beatrice of York (b.1988)

H.R.H. Princess Eugenie of York (b.1990)
History of titles:
19 Feb 1960 - 23 Jul 1986: H.R.H. The Prince Andrew
23 Jul 1986 - present: H.R.H. The Duke of York

H.R.H. Princess Beatrice of York
Granddaughter of the Queen
Born: 8 Aug 1988, Portland Hospital
        London
Full names: Beatrice Elizabeth Mary
Father: H.R.H. The Duke of York
Mother: Sarah Ferguson

H.R.H. Princess Eugenie of York

Granddaughter of the Queen
Born: 23 Mar 1990, Portland Hospital
        London
Full names: Eugenia Victoria Helena
Father: H.R.H. The Duke of York
Mother: Sarah Ferguson

Princess Eugenie's name is pronounced
yoo-zhen-ee

H.R.H. The Earl of Wessex
Son of the Queen
Born: 10 Mar 1964, Buckingham Palace
Full names: Edward Antony Richard
        Lewis
Full titles: Prince of the United Kingdom,
        Earl of Wessex, Viscount Severn
Father: H.R.H. The Duke of Edinburgh
Mother: H.M. The Queen
Married: 19 Jun 1999; St. George's
        Chapel, Windsor Castle

Wife: Sophie Rhys-Jones
Children:
Lady Louise Mountbatten-Windsor (b.2003)
James, Viscount Severn (b.2007
History of titles:
10 Mar 1964 - 19 Jun 1999: H.R.H. The Prince Edward
19 Jun 1999 - present: H.R.H. The Earl of Wessex

Counter to tradition, Prince Edward was not given a dukedom upon
his marriage. The unconfirmed story is that a family arrangement
has been made that when both the Queen and the Duke of
Edinburgh are dead, Charles, who will then be King, will re-create
the title Duke of Edinburgh for Edward.

In another contradiction to tradition, The Earl and Countess of
Wessex decided they wished their children to be styled as the
children of an Earl rather than as Prince and Princess, which is how
they are legally titled. In keeping with this, the son, James is styled
as Viscount Severn, following the tradition of styling heirs to Earls
(Dukes and Marquesses also) by their father's secondary titles, if
he has one.

H.R.H. The Countess of Wessex
Daughter-in-law of the Queen
Born: 20 Jan 1965, Oxford
Full names: Sophie Helen
Father: Christopher Rhys-Jones
Mother: Mary Sullivan
History of titles:
20 Jan 1965 - 19 Jun 1999: Miss Sophie
    Rhys-Jones
19 Jun 1999 - present: H.R.H. The
    Countess of Wessex

H.R.H. The Princess Royal
Daughter of the Queen
Born: 15 Aug 1950, Clarence House
    London
Full names: Anne Elizabeth Alice Mary
Father: H.R.H. The Duke of Edinburgh
Mother: H.M. The Queen
Married (1) 14 Nov 1973, Westminster
    Abbey (divorced 1992)
First Husband: Mark Phillips
Married (2) 12 Dec 1992, Crathie
Church near Balmoral
Second Husband: Timothy Laurence
Children (of 1st marriage):
Peter Phillips (b.1977)
Zara Phillips (b.1981)
History of titles:
15 Aug 1950 - 6 Feb 1952: H.R.H. Princess Anne of Edinburgh
6 Feb 1952 - 14 Nov 1973: H.R.H. The Princess Anne
14 Nov 1973 - 13 Jun 1987: H.R.H. The Princess Anne, Mrs. Mark
    Phillips
13 Jun 1987 - present: H.R.H. The Princess Royal

Princess Royal is a title somewhat unique among present day royal families, however it was inspired by the french royal family who called the King's eldest daughter Madame Royale. The practice was begun in Britain by King Charles I in 1642. The title is reserved for the eldest daughter of the Sovereign and is held for life. There can be only one Princess Royal at a time, so sometimes a princess has to wait until the previous holder dies before they can receive the honor. The last holder of the title was the Queen's aunt, Princess Louise, Countess of Harewood (daughter of George V) who died in 1965.

H.R.H. The Duke of Gloucester
1st cousin of the Queen (grandson of George V)
Born: 26 Aug 1944 Hadley Common, Hertfordshire
Full names: Richard Alexander Walter George
Full titles: Prince of Great Britain and Ireland, Duke of Gloucester, Earl of Ulster, Baron Cullenden
Father: H.R.H. the late Duke of Gloucester (The Prince Henry)
Mother: Lady Alice Montagu-Douglas-Scott
Married: 8 Jul 1972 Barwell, Northampton
Wife: Birgitte van Deurs
Children:
Alexander, Earl of Ulster (b.1974)
Lady Davina Lewis (née Windsor) (b.1977)
Lady Rose Gilman (née Windsor) (b.1980)
History of titles:
26 Aug 1944 - 10 Jun 1974: H.R.H. Prince Richard of Gloucester
10 Jun 1974 - present: H.R.H. The Duke of Gloucester

Gloucester is pronounced Glaw-ster

Prince Richard was his parent's second son. His elder brother, William, was killed when the plane he was piloting crashed during an air show in 1972.

His mother, Princess Alice, was given the honor of carrying her own given name in her widowhood by the Queen. Without this special consideration, she would have been styled as the Dowager Duchess of Gloucester after her husband's death. She lived to the age of 102 holding the record for longest living British royal. She carried out royal duties into her late 90s.

H.R.H. The Duchess of Gloucester
Wife of 1st cousin of the Queen
Born: 20 Jun 1946, Odense
    Denmark
Full names: Birgitte Eva
Father: Asger Henriksen
Mother: Vivian van Deurs
History of titles:
20 Jun 1946 - 15 Jan 1966: Miss
    Birgitte Henriksen
15 Jan 1966 - 8 Jul 1972: Miss
    Birgitte van Deurs
8 Jul 1972 - 10 Jun 1974: H.R.H.
    Princess Richard of Gloucester
10 Jun 1974 - present: H.R.H. The Duchess of Gloucester

Birgitte took her mother's name after her parent separated.

H.R.H. The Duke of Kent
1st cousin to the Queen (grandson of
    George V)
Born: 9 Oct 1935, London
Full names: Edward George
    Nicholas Paul Patrick
Full titles: Prince of Great Britain
    and Ireland, Duke of Kent, Earl
    of St. Andrews, Baron
    Downpatrick
Father: H.R.H. the late Duke of
    Kent (The Prince George)
Mother: H.R.H. Princess Marina of
    Greece
Married: 8 Jun 1961, York
Wife: Katherine Worsley

Children:
George, Earl of St. Andrew (b.1962)
Lady Helen Taylor (b.1964)
Lord Nicholas Windsor (b.1970)

History of titles:
9 Oct 1935 - 25 Aug 1942: H.R.H. Prince Edward of Kent
25 Aug 1942 - present: H.R.H. The Duke of Kent

Through his mother, the Duke is closely related to the royal families of Greece and Russia.

Although his wife has converted to Catholicism, he retains his place in succession because she was Protestant when he married her. His younger son and the elder two children of his elder son have also converted to Catholicism and are not longer in the line of succession. This also applies to his son and heir, Lord St. Andrews because he married a Catholic. Their religion does not affect their ability to inherit the Dukedom though.

H.R.H. The Duchess of Kent
Wife of 1st cousin of the Queen
Born: 22 Feb 1933, Hovingham, Yorkshire
Full names: Katharine Lucy Mary
Father: Sir William Worsley, Baronet
Mother: Joyce Brunner
History of titles:
22 Feb 1933 - 8 Jun 1961: Miss Katharine
    Worsley
8 Jun 1961 - present: H.R.H. The Duchess of
Kent

The Duchess chooses not to use H.R.H. and prefers to be introduced as Katherine, Duchess of Kent, but her formal style remains H.R.H. The Duchess of Kent.

The Duchess has suffered declining health in recent years and has reduced her royal duties since 2002.

H.R.H. Prince Michael of Kent
1st cousin of the Queen (grandson of
   George V)
Born: 4 Jul 1942, Coppins, Iver,
   Buckinghamshire
Full names: Michael George Charles
   Franklin
Father: H.R.H. the late Duke of Kent (The
   Prince George)
Mother: H.R.H. Princess Marina of Greece
Married: 30 Jun 1978 Vienna (civil) and 30 Oct 1978 Westminster
   Abby (religious)
Wife: Baroness Marie-Christine von Reibnitz)
Children:
Lord Frederick Windsor (b.1979)
Lady Gabriella (Ella) Windsor (b.1981)

Prince Michael lost his place in the line of succession when he
married, since his wife is Catholic. They have raised their children
in the Anglican church so they remain in succession.

H.R.H. Princess Michael of Kent
Wife of 1st cousin of the Queen
Born: 15 Jan 1945, Karlovy Vary, Czech
   Republic (formerly Karlsbad)
Full name: Marie-Christine Agnes Hedwig
   Ida
Father: Baron Günther von Reibnitz
Mother: Countess Maria Anna Szapáry
Married (1) 14 Sep 1971 London (divorced
   1977, annulled 1978)
First husband: Thomas Troubridge (no
   issue)
Married (2) 30 Jun 1978 Vienna (civil) and 30 Oct 1978
   Westminster Abbey (religious)
Second husband: H.R.H. Prince Michael of Kent
History of titles:
15 Jan 1945 - 14 Sep 1971: Baroness Marie-Christine von Reibnitz

14 Sep 1971 - 30 Jun 1978: Mrs. Thomas Troubridge
30 Jun 1978 - present: H.R.H. Princess Michael of Kent

H.R.H. Princess Alexandra, The Hon. Lady Ogilvy
Born: 25 Dec 1936, London
Full names: Alexandra Helen Elizabeth Olga
    Christabel
Father: H.R.H. the late Duke of Kent (The
    Prince George)
Mother: H.R.H. Princess Marina of Greece
Married: 24 Apr 1963, Westminster Abbey
Husband: Hon. Sir Angus Ogilvy KCVO
(d.2004)

Children:
James Ogilvy (b.1964)
Mrs. Marina Mowatt (b.1966)
History of titles:
25 Dec 1936 - 24 Apr 1963: H.R.H. Princess Alexandra of Kent
24 Apr 1963 - 31 Dec 1988: H.R.H. Princess Alexandra, The Hon .
    Mrs. Angus Ogilvy
31 Dec 1988 - present: H.R.H. Princess Alexandra, The Hon. Lady
    Ogilvy

Princess Alexandra went from Mrs. Angus Ogilvy to Lady Ogilvy
when her late husband was knighted with the Royal Victorian
Order 31 Dec 1988.

Other members of the Queen's Family

Vice-Admiral Timothy Laurence (b.1955) husband of the
Princess Royal. He is the Princess's second husband and step-
father to her children by her first husband, Mark Phillips.

Peter Phillips (b.1977) grandson of the Queen, son of The
Princess Royal. He is the Queen's first grandchild and was the first
one to marry. He is also father of the Queen's first great-
grandchild, **Savannah Phillips** (b.2010). His wife is **Autumn
Phillips** (b.1978 née Kelly) whom he married in 2008 in

St.George's Chapel, Windsor Castle. Peter and Autumn expect their second child in March, 2012.

Zara Phillips (b.1981) granddaughter of the Queen, daughter of The Princess Royal. An accomplished competitive equestrian. She married rugby player **Mike Tindall** on 30 Jul 2011 in Edinburgh.

David, Viscount Linley (b.1961) nephew of the Queen, son of the late Princess Margaret. His father is Antony Armstrong-Jones, Earl of Snowden, the famous photographer. David is styled Viscount Linley as a courtesy title which denotes he is the heir to his father. Lord Linley married in 1993 **Serena Stanhope** (b.1970) whose father is now the Earl of Harrington. At the time of the wedding she was styled as The Hon. Serena Stanhope because her father had not yet inherited the Earldom and was still styled as Viscount Petersham. Lord and Lady Linley have two children: **Hon. Charles Armstrong-Jones** (b.1999) and **Hon. Margarita Armstrong Jones** (b.2002)

Lady Sarah Chatto (b.1964) née Lady Sarah Armstrong-Jones; niece of the Queen, daughter of the late Princess Margaret. She gained worldwide notice as the chief bridesmaid at the wedding of Lady Diana Spencer to the Prince of Wales. She married **Daniel Chatto** in 1994. They have two children: **Samuel Chatto** (b.1996) and **Arthur Chatto** (b.1999)

Photo Acknowledgements
The photo of the Queen is courtesy *The Buckingham Palace Press Office*
All other photos in the section are from the author's collection.

Liechtenstein

Current Sovereign: His Serene Highness Hans-Adams II, Prince of Liechtenstein.

Full Titles: Reigning Prince of Liechtenstein, Duke of Troppau and Jägerndorf, Count zu Rietberg, Sovereign of the House of Liechtenstein

Quick Life Facts:
Born: 14 Feb 1945 Zürich, Switzerland
Full names: Johannes (Hans-) Adam Ferdinand Alois Josef Maria
    Marko d'Aviano Pius
Father: H.S.H. Franz Joseph II, Prince of Liechtenstein
Mother: Countess Georgine (Gina) von Wilczek
Married: 30 Jul 1967 Vaduz
Wife: Countess Marie Kinsky von Wchinitz und Tettau
Ascended the Throne: 13 Nov 1989
Took Oath of Office: 15 Aug 1990
Children:
H.S.H. Hereditary Prince Alois of Liechtenstein (b.1968)
H.S.H. Prince Maximilian of Liechtenstein (b.1969)
H.S.H. Prince Constantin of Liechtenstein (b.1972)
Princess Tatjana, Frau von Lattorf (b.1973)
History of titles:
14 Feb 1945 - 13 Nov 1989: H.S.H. Hereditary Prince Hans-

Adams of Liechtenstein
13 Nov 1989 - present: H.S.H. The Prince of Liechtenstein

The Liechtenstein monarchy in a nutshell:
Liechtenstein is a principality so it technically does not have a royal family, but a princely family. The same is true of the other things that tend to be called "Royal" when associated with a Kingdom: the palaces, the jewels, the crown, etc. When speaking of Liechtenstein, or any other principality, the correct word to use is Princely rather than Royal.

Liechtenstein is unique among European monarchies in that the country was named for the family and not vice versa. In 1719, Anton Florian von Liechtenstein purchased the county of Vaduz and the lordship of Schellenberg from the Hohenems family. Emperor Charles VI granted him the title and rank of a Sovereign Prince, beginning the country of Liechtenstein.

There are several male lines of descent from Anton Florian, creating numerous Princes of Liechtenstein. Membership of the Princely Family is limited to the male-line descendants of Prince Johann I (1760-1835), However, the duties of the Princely Family are today only carried out by the Sovereign Prince, his wife, his heir and his heir's wife.

In 2004, Prince Hans-Adams turned the day-to-day governmental duties over to his son, Hereditary Prince Alois, but remains the Head of State.

Titles in the Princely Family:
All members of the family are titled Prince or Princess of Liechtenstein, Count or Countess von Rietberg. The Sovereign and his wife are styled The Prince and Princess of Liechtenstein and the heir-apparent and his wife are styled Hereditary Prince and Hereditary Princess of Liechtenstein. There have been cases where a Prince has married without the consent of the Sovereign in which case his wife and children were not entitled to be Prince or Princess. In these cases, the Sovereign is to decide what surname and title, if any, the wife and children are to carry. The

Constitution of Liechtenstein expressly forbids adopted people to be members of the Princely House, however it does allow illegitimate children who are legitimated by the subsequent marriage of their parents to be House members.

Succession:
The line of Succession is limited to the males who desend in male-line only from Prince Johann I which now total dozens of Princes. The first 10 are listed here.
The Line of Succession:
1. H.S.H. Hereditary Price Alois
2. H.S.H Prince Joseph Wenzel
3. H.S.H. Prince Georg
4. H.S.H. Prince Nikolaus
5. H.S.H. Prince Maximilian
6. H.S.H. Prince Alfons
7. H.S.H. Prince Constantin
8. H.S.H. Prince Moritz
9. H.S.H. Prince Benedikt
10. H.S.H. Prince Philipp Erasmus

Members of the Princely Family

H.S.H. The Princess of Liechtenstein
Wife of the Sovereign Prince
Born: 14 Apr 1940 Prague
Full names: Marie Aglaë
Father: Count Ferdinand Kinsky von
    Wchinitz und Tettau
Mother: Countess Henriette von Ledebur-
    Wicheln
History of titles:
    14 Apr 1940 - 30 Jul 1967: Countess Marie
Kinsky von Wchinitz und Tettau
30 Jul 1967 - 13 Nov 1989: H.S.H. Hereditary Princess Marie of
    Liechtenstein
13 Nov - present: H.S.H. The Princess of Liechtenstein

H.S.H. Hereditary Prince Alois of Liechtenstein
Son and heir of the Sovereign Prince
Born: 11 Jun 1968 Zürich
Full names: Alois Philipp Maria
Father: H.S.H. The Prince of Liechtenstein
Mother: Countess Marie Kinsky von
    Wchnitz und Tettau
Married: 3 Jul 1993 Vaduz
Wife: H.R.H. Princess Sophie of Bavaria,
Duchess in Bavaria

Children:
H.S.H. Prince Josef Wenzel of Liechtenstein (b.1995)
H.S.H. Princess Marie-Caroline of Liechtenstein (b.1996)
H.S.H. Prince Georg of Liechtenstein (b.1999)
H.S.H. Prince Nikolaus of Liechtenstein (b.2000)

H.R.H. Hereditary Princess Sophie of Liechtenstein
Daughter-in-law of the Sovereign Prince
Born: 28 Oct 1967 Munich
Full name: Sophie Elizabeth Marie
    Gabrielle
Father: Prince Max of Bavaria, Duke in
    Bavaria
Mother: Countess Elizabeth Douglas

Hereditary Princess Sophie's family are members of the Royal Family of Bavaria. In additon to the royal line, there was also a line of Dukes in Bavaria which became extinct in 1973. Duke Ludwig Wilhelm adopted Sophie's father, Prince Max, to be his heir, giving Max's family the double title Prince/Princess of Bavaria and Duke/Duchess in Bavaria. And since her previous title was of a higher rank than her married title, she retains the predicate H.R.H. which went with Princess of Bavaria

The Hereditary Princess also holds another interesting place in British history. She will eventually be the heiress to the House of Stuart which was deposed from the English and Scottish Thrones in the 1680's. That line of descent took a complicated path through serveral royal houses via several princesses before currently landing on Franz, Duke of Bavaria, also claimant to the former Bavarian Throne. Duke Franz is the childless uncle of Princess Sophie. Sophie's father is Franz's heir and Sophie is Max's eldest daughter. So, having no brothers, Sophie will one day inherit the Stuart claim (also called the Jacobite claim) and then pass it on to he son Prince Joseph Wenzel. This brings about the interesting fact that the future Prince of tiny Liechtenstein will also have a claim to the mighty British Empire.

Other Members of the Princely Family

H.S.H. Prince Maximilian of Liechtenstein (b.1969) Son of the Sovereign Prince. Married **Angela Brown** in 2000 and is the father of **Prince Alfons** (b.2001)

H.S.H. Prince Constantin of Liechtenstein (b.1972) Son of the Sovereign Prince. Married **Countess Maria Kálnoky** in 1999. They have three children: **Moritz** (b.2003), **Georgina** (b.2005), and **Benedikt** (*2008)

Frau Tatjana von Lattorff (b.1973) Daughter of the Sovereign Prince. Married **Philipp von Lattorff** in 1999. They have seven children: **Lukas** (b.2000), **Elisabeth** (b.2002), **Marie** (b.2004), **Camilla** (b.2005), **Anna** (b.2007), **Sophie** (b.2009), and **Maximilian** (b.2011)

H.S.H. Prince Philipp Erasmus of Liechtenstein (b.1946) Brother of the Sovereign Prince. Married **Isabelle de l'Arbre de Malander** in 1971. Their eldest son **Alexander** (b.1972) is the only one married. His wife is **Astrid Kohl** and their only child is **Princess Theodora** (b.2004) . Philipp Erasmus and Isabelle's other children are **Wenzeslaus** (b.1974) and **Rudolf** (b.1975)

H.S.H. Prince Nikolaus of Liechtenstein (b.1947) Brother of the Sovereign Prince. Married **Princess Margarethe of Luxembourg**, sister of the current Grand Duke. Their surviving children are: **Maria-Annunciata** (b.1985), **Marie-Astrid** (b.1987), and **Josef-Emanuel** (b.1989). Their eldest child, Leopold, died the day of his birth.

H.S.H. Princess Nora, Marquesa de Mariño (b.1950) Sister of the Sovereign Prince and widow of **Don Vicente Sartorius, Marqués de Mariño** (d.2002). Their daughter is **Doña Maria Teresa Sartorius y de Liechtenstein** (b.1992)

Photo Credits:
All photos are courtesy *www.fuerstenhaus.li*

Luxembourg

Current Sovereign: H.R.H. Henri, Grand Duke of Luxembourg

Quick Life Facts:
Born: 16 Apr 1955 Betzdorf Castle, Luxembourg
Full names: Henri Albert Gabriel Félix Marie Guillaume
Full titles: Grand Duke of Luxembourg, Duke of Nassau, Count of
    the Rhine, Count of Sayn, Königstein, Katzenelnbogen, and
    Diez, Viscount of Hammerstein, Lord of Mahlberg,
    Wiesbaden, Idstein, Merenberg, Limbourg, and Eppstein
Father; H.R.H. Grand Duke Jean of Luxembourg
Mother: H.R.H. Princess Josephine-Charlotte of Belgium
Married: 4 Feb 1981 Luxembourg
Wife: Maria Teresa Mestre
Children:
H.R.H. Hereditary Grand Duke Guillaume of Luxembourg
    (b.1981)
H.R.H. Prince Félix of Luxembourg (b.1984)
H.R.H. Prince Louis of Luxembourg (b.1986)
H.R.H. Princess Alexandra of Luxembourg (b.1991)
H.R.H. Prince Sébastian of Luxembourg (b.1992)
Ascended Throne: 7 Oct 2000
Took Oath: 7 Oct 2000
History of titles:
16 Apr 1955 - 12 Nov 1964: H.R.H. Prince Henri of Luxembourg
12 Nov 1964 - 7 Oct 2000: H.R.H. Hereditary Grand Duke Henri
    of Luxembourg

7 Oct 2000 - present: H.R.H. The Grand Duke of Luxembourg

Luxembourgish monarchy in a nutshell:
The original House of Luxembourg was founded in 963 by a Count of Ardennes. That house became extinct in the male line in 1437, but not before producing three Holy Roman Emperors. The County of Luxembourg was then sold to the Duke of Burgundy and remained with his dominions until the end of the Napoleonic Empire in 1815. The Congress of Vienna, which had the task of redrawing the map of Europe, reformed Luxembourg into a Grand Duchy and gave it to the Netherlands. The Kings of the Netherlands were also styled Grand Dukes of Luxembourg until 1890.

The succession laws in Luxembourg in 1890 were different than the Netherlands. While the Netherlands allowed female succession, Luxembourg only allowed it upon the complete extinction of the House of Nassau. Therefore when Queen Wilhelmina succeeded in the Netherlands, Luxembourg went to the next male, Adolf, Duke of Nassau, who became Grand Duke Adolphe. The male lines of Nassau did finally reach complete extinction when Adolphe's son, Guillaume IV died in 1912. After a brief reign by his eldest daughter, Marie-Adelaide, the Throne fell to his 2nd daughter, Charlotte.

All members of the Grand Ducal Family living today are descended from Charlotte and her husband, Prince Felix of Bourbon-Parma.

Abdication has become common place in Luxembourg. Grand Duchess Marie-Adelaide abdicated in 1919 following World War I, mostly for political reasons. In 1964, as Grand Duchess Charlotte was getting to be older, she abdicated so her son, Jean could have a full reign. Grand Duke Jean himself abdicated for the same reasons in 2000.

Luxembourg is a Grand Duchy, so it technically does not have a "Royal" Family, but rather a Grand Ducal Family. Same with other "royal" items like castles, the court, and jewels, they are all grand ducal and not royal.

Titles of the Grand Ducal Family:
The titles of the family have changed often. When Adolphe became Grand Duke, he was styled H.R.H. The Grand Duke and other family members were styled His or Her Grand Ducal Highness (H.G.D.H.) Prince or Princess of Luxembourg, Prince or Princess of Nassau. These titles remain, to some extent, today. The descendants of Grand Duchess Charlotte, by virtue of her marriage to Prince Felix, got upgraded to Royal Highnesses and gained the additional title Prince or Princess of Bourbon-Parma. In 1987, Grand Duke Jean formally discontinued the use of Bourbon-Parma for himself and his descendants, but they kept Royal Highness.

Today the family titles are dictated by a Grand-Ducal Decree issued on 21 Sep 1995. Now the title Prince or Princess of Luxembourg is restricted to the children of the Grand Duke and the children of the heir-apparent. Further descendants are to be titled Prince or Princess of Nassau, still with Royal Highness. Children of an unapproved marriage are to be titled Count or Countess de Nassau.

When Grand Duke Jean abdicated in 2000, it was decreed by his son that he would be styled as "Grand Duke Jean of Luxembourg" for the rest of his life, which is different from being the THE Grand Duke of Luxembourg which indicates the current Sovereign.

The heir-apparent is traditionally titled Hereditary Grand Duke, however this title is not automatic upon becoming the heir-apparent. It must be created in each instance by the Sovereign. The current Hereditary Grand Duke became heir-apparent in October 2000 but was not created the title Hereditary Grand Duke until December of that year.

There have been several cases of marriages not being approved at their onset, only to be later approved and to have the children upgraded. Those will be discussed with each affected individuals profile.

Name of the Grand Ducal Family:
Although patrilineally descended from the Bourbon-Parma family, the House and Family name has remained "of Nassau".

Succession:
On 20 Jun 2011, the Grand Duke announced that the succession, beginning with his direct descendants, will allow female succession and that children will be in line regardless of gender. The Grand Duke's next younger brother and the Grand Duke's 3rd son have renounced succession rights for themselves and their descendants.

The Line of Succession:
1. H.R.H. Hereditary Grand Duke Guillaume (b.1981)
2. H.R.H. Prince Félix of Luxembourg (b.1984)
3. H.R.H. Princess Alexandra of Luxembourg (b.1991)
4. H.R.H. Prince Sébastian of Luxembourg (b.1992)
5. H.R.H. Prince Guillaume of Luxembourg (b.1963)
6. H.R.H. Prince Paul Louis of Nassau (b.1998)
7. H.R.H. Prince Léopold of Nassau (b.2000)
8. H.R.H. Prince Jean André of Nassau (b.2004)

Grand Ducal Family Members

H.R.H. The Grand Duchess of Luxembourg
Wife of the Grand Duke
Born: 22 Mar 1956 Havana, Cuba
Full names: Maria Teresa
Father: José Antonio Mestre Alvarez
Mother: María Teresa Batista Falla
History of titles:
22 Mar 1956 - 4 Feb 1981: Maria Teresa
    Mestre Batista
4 Feb 1981 - 7 Oct 2000: H.R.H. Hereditary Grand Duchess Maria
    Teresa of Luxembourg
7 Oct 2000 - present: H.R.H. The Grand Duchess of Luxembourg

H.R.H. Grand Duke Jean of Luxembourg
Father of the Grand Duke
Born: 5 Jan 1921 Berg Castle, Colmar-Berg
Full names: Jean Benoît Guillaume Robert
Antoine Louis Marie Adolphe Marc
d'Aviano
Current titles: Grand Duke Jean of
Luxembourg, Prince of Nassau
Father: H.R.H. Prince Felix of Bourbon-Parma
Mother: H.R.H. Charlotte, Grand Duchess of
Luxembourg
Married: 9 Apr 1953 Luxembourg
Wife: H.R.H. Princess Josephine-Charlotte of Belgium (d.2005)
Children:
H.I. & R.H Archduchess Marie Astrid of Austria (b.1954)
H.R.H. The Grand Duke of Luxembourg (b.1955)
H.R.H. Prince Jean of Luxembourg (b.1957) (twin)
H.R.H. Princess Margaretha of Liechtenstein (b.1957) (twin)
H.R.H. Prince Guillaume of Luxembourg (b.1963)
History of titles:
5 Jan 1921 - 5 Jan 1939; H.R.H. Prince Jean of Luxembourg
5 Jan 1939 - 12 Nov 1964; H.R.H. Hereditary Grand Duke Jean of
Luxembourg
12 Nov 1964 - 7 Oct 2000: H.R.H. The Grand Duke of
Luxembourg
7 Oct 2000 - present: H.R.H. Grand Duke Jean of Luxembourg

**H.R.H. Hereditary Grand Duke Guillaume
of Luxembourg**
Son and heir-apparent of the Grand Duke
Born: 11 Nov 1981 Luxembourg
Full names: Guillaume Jean Joseph Marie
Father: H.R.H. The Grand Duke of
Luxembourg
Mother: Maria Teresa Mestre Batista
History of titles:
11 Nov 1981 - 18 Dec 2000: H.R.H. Prince
Guillaume of Luxembourg
18 Dec 2000 - present: H.R.H. Hereditary Grand Duke Guillaume

of Luxembourg

When he becomes Grand Duke he will be Guillaume V, their first three of that name were Kings Willem I, II, and III of the Netherlands.

H.R.H. Prince Félix of Luxembourg
Son of the Grand Duke
Born: 3 Jun 1984 Luxembourg
Full names: Félix Léopold Marie Guillaume
Father: H.R.H. The Grand Duke of
    Luxembourg
Mother: Maria Teresa Mestre Batista

H.R.H. Prince Louis of Luxembourg
Son of the Grand Duke
Born: 3 Aug 1986 Luxembourg
Full names: Louis Xavier Marie Guillaume
Father: H.R.H. The Grand Duke of
    Luxembourg
Mother: Maria Teresa Mestre Batista
Married: 29 Sep 2006 Gilsdorf, Luxembourg
Wife: Tessy Antony

Children:
H.R.H. Prince Gabriel of Nassau (b.2006)
H.R.H. Prince Noah of Nassau (b.2007)

Prince Louis renounced his succession rights and those of his children upon his marriage.

H.R.H. Princess Tessy of Luxembourg
Daughter-in-law of the Grand Duke
Born: 28 Oct 1985 Luxembourg
Father: François Antony
Mother: Régine Heidemann
History of titles:
28 Oct 1985 - 29 Sep 2006: Mademoiselle
    Tessy Antony
29 Sep 2006 - 23 Jun 2009: Madame Tessy de
    Nassau
23 Jun 2009 - present: H.R.H. Princess Tessy of Luxembourg

Princess Tessy and her children were originally given the surname de Nassau without a title but were granted full titles 23 Jun 2009

H.R.H. Princess Alexandra of Luxembourg
Daugher of the Grand Duke
Born: 16 Feb 1991 Luxembourg
Full names: Alexandra Joséphine Teresa
    Charlotte Marie Wilhelmine
Father: H.R.H. The Grand Duke of
    Luxembourg
Mother: Maria Teresa Mestre Batista

Princess Alexandra was added to the succession in June 2011 when her father decreed a gender blind succession.

H.R.H. Prince Sébastian of Luxembourg
Son of the Grand Duke
Born: 16 Apr 1992 Luxembourg
Full names: Sébastian Henri Marie Guillaume
Father: H.R.H. The Grand Duke of
    Luxembourg
Mother: Maria Teresa Mestre Batista

H.R.H. Prince Guillaume of Luxembourg
Brother of the Grand Duke
Born: 1 May 1963 Betzdorf Castle,
    Luxembourg
Full names: Guillaume Marie Louis Christian
Father: H.R. H. Grand Duke Jean of
    Luxembourg
Mother: H.R.H. Princess Josephine Charlotte
    of Belgium
Married: 24 Sep 1994 Versailles, France
Wife: Sibilla Weiller
Children:
H.R.H. Prince Paul-Louis of Nassau (b.1996)
H.R.H. Prince Léopold of Nassau (b.2000) (twin)
H.R.H. Princess Charlotte of Nassau (b.2000) (twin)
H.R.H. Prince Jean André of Nassau (b.2004) (twin)

In September 2000, Prince Guillaume and his wife were involved in a bad car crash. Guillaume's skull was fractured and severe damage was done to his face. Plastic surgery has now mostly restored his face, and the permanent damage to his brain has been minimal.

Princess Sibilla is a great-granddaughter of King Alfonso XIII of Spain, making her a second cousin to King Juan Carlos.

H.I. & R.H. Archduchess Marie Astrid of Austria
Sister of the Grand Duke
Born: 17 Feb 1954 Betzdorf Castle,
    Luxembourg
Full names: Marie Astrid Liliane Charlotte
    Léopoldine Wilhelmine Ingeborg Antonia
    Élisabeth Anne Alberte
Full titles: Princess of Luxembourg, Princess
    of Nassau, Archduchess of Austria,
    Princess of Hungary and Bohemia

Father: H.R.H. Grand Duke Jean of Luxembourg
Mother: H.R.H. Princess Josephine-Charlotte of Belgium
Married: 6 Feb 1982 Luxembourg
Husband: H.I. & R.H. Archduke Carl Christian of Austria
Children:
H.I. & R.H. Archduchess Marie Christine of Austria (b.1979)
H.I. & R.H. Archduke Imre of Austria (b.1985)
H.I. & R.H. Archduke Christoph of Austria (b.1988)
H.I. & R.H. Archduke Alexander of Austria (b.1990)
H.I. & R.H. Archduchess Gabriella of Austria (b.1994)
History of titles:
17 Feb 1954 - 6 Feb 1982: H.R.H. Princess Marie Astrid of
    Luxembourg
6 Feb 1982 - present: H.I. & R.H. Archduchess Marie Astrid of
    Austria

Archduchess Marie Astrid's husband is a grandson of Karl I, the
last Emperor of the Austro-Hungarian Empire.

H.R.H. Princess Margaretha of Liechtenstein
Sister of the Grand Duke
Born: 15 May 1957 Betzdorf Castle,
    Luxembourg
Full names: Margaretha Antonia Marie Félicité
Full titles: Princess of Luxembourg, Princess of
    Nassau, Princess of Liechtenstein, Countess
    zu Rietberg
Father: H.R.H. Grand Duke Jean of
    Luxembourg
Mother: H.R.H. Princess Josephine Charlotte of Belgium
Married: 20 Mar 1982 Luxembourg
Husband: H.S.H. Prince Nikolaus of Liechtenstein
Children:
H.S.H. Prince Leopold of Liechtenstein (b.&d.1984)
H.S.H. Princess Maria Anunciata of Liechtenstein (b.1985)
H.S.H. Princess Marie-Astrid of Liechtenstein (b.1987)
H.S.H. Prince Josef-Emanuel of Liechtenstein (b.1989)
History of titles:
15 May 1957 - 20 Mar 1982: H.R.H. Princess Margaretha of

Luxembourg

20 Mar 1982 - present: H.R.H. Princess Margaretha of
     Liechtenstein

Princess Margaretha's husband is a brother of the Sovereign Prince
of Liechtenstein. She is a twin to her brother, Prince Jean.

Other Family Members

H.R.H. Prince Jean of Luxembourg (b.1957) Renounced his
succession rights in 1986 and has since married twice without
permission. His children are titled H.R.H. Prince/Princess of
Nassau. By his first wife, Hélène Vestur, he has **Princess Marie-
Gabrielle** (b.1986), **Prince Constantine** (b.1988), **Prince
Wenceslaus** (b.1990), and **Prince Carl-Johan** (b.1992). Jean is
currently married to Diane de Guerre.

**H.R.H. Princess Marie-Gabrielle, Dowager Landgravine of
Holstein-Ledreborg** (b.1925) Aunt of the Grand Duke. Widow of
Knud, Landgrave (Lehnsgreve in Danish) **of Holstein-
Ledreborg**, she has five daughters, the forth of whom, Silvia,
administers the family castle at Ledreborg, Denmark.

H.R.H. The Dowager Princess of Ligne (b.1929) Aunt of the
Grand Duke. Born Princess Alix of Luxembourg, she is the widow
of **Antoine, Prince of Ligne** (d.2005). Two of her seven children,
Michel, the current Prince and Princess Christine are married to
members of the Brazilian royal family. Her grandson, Prince Pedro
Luiz of Brazil was killed in the crash of Air France flight 447 in
2009.

H.R.H. Princess Charlotte of Nassau (b.1967) First cousin of the
Grand Duke, daughter of Prince Charles of Luxembourg (d.1977).
Married since 1993 to **Marc-Victor Cunningham**, she has three
children.

H.R.H. Prince Robert of Nassau (b.1968) First cousin of the
Grand Duke, son of Prince Charles of Luxembourg (d.1977).

Married since 1994 to Julie Ongaro, he too has three children: **Princess Charlotte** (b.1995), **Prince Alexandre** (b.1997), and **Prince Frederik** (b.2002).

Photo Credits:
Photos of the Grand Duke, Grand Duchess, Hereditary Grand Duke and Grand Duke Jean, are courtesy *the Grand-Ducal press office*. All other photos are courtesy *PressRoyal*.

Monaco

Current Sovereign: H.S.H. Albert II, Prince of Monaco

Quick Life Facts:
Born: 14 Mar 1958 Monaco
Full names: Albert Alexandre Louis Pierre
Full titles: Prince of Monaco, Duke of Valentinois, Marquis de Baux, Count de Carladès, Count de Polignac, Baron de Calvinet, Baron de Buis, Lord de Saint-Rémy, Sire de Montignon, Count de Torigni, Baron de Saint-Lô, Baron de La Luthumière, Baron de Hambye, Duke of Estouteville, Duke of Mazarin, Duke of Mayene, Prince of Château-Porcien, Count de Ferrette, Count de Belfort, Count de Thann, Count de Rosemont, Baron d'Altkirch, Lord d'Isenheim, Marquis de Chilly, Count de Longjumeau, Baron de Massy, Marquis de Guiscard
Father: H.S.H. Rainier III, Prince of Monaco
Mother: Grace Kelly
Married: 1 (civil) & 2 July 2011, Princely Palace Monaco
Ascended Throne: 6 Apr 2005
Enthroned: 12 Jul 2005
<u>Children</u> (illegitimate):

by Tamara Rotolo:
Jazmin Grimaldi (b.1992)
by Nicole Coste:
Alexandre Coste (b.2003)
History of titles:
14 Mar 1958 - 6 Apr 2005: H.S.H. The Hereditary Prince of
Monaco
6 Apr 2005 - present: H.S.H. The Prince of Monaco

Monegasque monarchy in a nutshell:
Monaco is a principality so it has a Princely Family, Princely
Palace, Princely Weddings, not Royal Family, etc.

Monaco has been ruled by the Grimaldi family since 1297 when
Francesco Grimaldi took control of the small territory. They were
first titled Lords of Monaco as a Protectorate of several Duchies
and Kingdoms along the way. In 1633, Honoré II managed to have
Monaco recognized as a Sovereign principality and assumed the
title Prince.

Although Grimaldis have ruled Monaco for over 700 years, the
male line has not been maintained. Prince Antoine I's death
brought the male-line to an end. His daughter, Louise Hippolyte,
became Monaco's only Sovereign Princess. She married Jacques
Goyon de Matignon, but named her children all Grimaldi so the
name would continue.

This second House of Grimaldi died out with Prince Louis II in
1949. Prince Louis had an illegitimate daughter, Charlotte, but no
other children. His next heir was a cousin, the German Duke of
Urach. World War II made the prospect of a German Prince of
Monaco unthinkable so Prince Louis solved the problem by legally
adopting his illegitimate daughter and making her son his heir.
Charlotte was married to Count Pierre Polignac, but raised her two
children with the name Grimaldi. Their son became Prince Rainier
III, the father of the current Sovereign Prince.

Monaco had long escaped the notice of most of the world. It
became a secret hideout for many a criminal and its topography

was appealing to those who wished not to be found. Monaco sits on a harbor and its inland border is very mountainous. Prince Louis begun the process of reforming Monaco's citizenry and its reputation. He arranged for a railway to be built to Monaco and established a high-end vacation resort destination at the end of the rail line. He circulated through the European resorts encouraging Europe's royal and noble classes to come visit his tiny Principality. Later, his grandson used a well-trained semi-militia police force to drive out the criminal elements and create the paradise resort it is today.

Monaco got world wide attention when Prince Rainier met and fell in love with Oscar-winning actress Grace Kelly. After a year-long courtship, Grace left Hollywood behind to become the Princess of Monaco, becoming Europe's first "fairy-tale princess" when her wedding was televised live and also re-broadcast all over the world.

The lives of Monaco's princely family played out in the era of television. In keeping with the lifestyle of Monaco, their children became known for fast living. Then tragedy struck in 1982 when Princess Grace and her daughter Stephanie went off the road in the mountains over Monaco. Grace was killed and Stephanie seriously injured. Ill fate befell the family a second time 8 years later when Princess Caroline's husband was killed in an accident during a boat race.

Prince Rainier's death in 2005, followed by his only sibling, Princess Antoinette, have shrunk the Princely Family down to only the current Prince, his sisters and their children.

Titles within the Princely Family:
Members of the family are titled Prince or Princess of Monaco with the predicate His or Her Serene Highness. The heir-apparent also carries the additional title Marquis de Baux.

Succession:
In 2002, the law of succession was changed to limit the succession to the legitimate descendants of the Sovereign Prince or Princess

and those of his or her siblings. It also allowed for the succession of females, but preserves the preference of males amongst siblings. Being a little more liberal than most succession laws, Monaco does allow for the succession of an illegitimate child, but only if that child's parents later married legitimating the child.

Line of Succession:
1. H.R.H. The Princess of Hanover
2. Andrea Casiraghi
3. Pierre Casiraghi
4. Charlotte Casiraghi
5. H.R.H. Princess Alexandra of Hanover
6. H.S.H. Princess Stephanie of Monaco
7. Louis Ducruet
8. Pauline Ducruet

Members of the Princely Family

H.S.H. The Princess of Monaco
Wife of the Sovereign Prince
Born: 25 Jan 1978, Bulawayo, South Africa
Full names: Charlene Lynette
Father: Michael Wittstock
Mother: Lynette Humberstone
History of Titles:
25 Jan 1978 - 1 Jul 2011: Miss Charlene Wittstock
1 Jul 2011 - present: H.S.H. The Princess of Monaco

H.R.H. The Princess of Hanover
Sister and heiress-presumptive of the Sovereign Prince
Born: 23 Jan 1957 Monaco
Full names: Caroline Louise Marguerite
Father: H.S.H. Rainier III, Prince of Monaco
Mother: Grace Kelly
Married (1): 29 Jun 1978 Monaco (divorced 1980)

First husband: Philippe Junot
Married (2): 29 Dec 1983 Monaco
Second husband: Stefano Casiraghi (d.1990)
Married (3): 23 Jan 1999 Monaco (civil) & 27 Jan 1999
Marienburg, Germany (religious)
Third Husband: H.R.H. The Prince of Hanover
Children:
by 2nd husband (none by 1st):
Andrea Casiraghi (b.1984)
Charlotte Casiraghi (b.1986)
Pierre Casiraghi (b.1987)
by 3rd husband:
H.R.H. Princess Alexandra of Hanover (b.1999)
History of titles:
23 Jan 1957 - 23 Jan 1997: H.S.H. Princess Caroline of Monaco
23 Jan 1997 - present: H.R.H. The Princess of Hanover

H.R.H. The Prince of Hanover
Brother-in-law of the Sovereign Prince
Born: 26 Feb 1956 Hannover, Germany
Full names: Ernst August Albert Otto
    Rupprecht Oskar Berthold Friedrich-
    Ferdinand Christian-Ludwig
Full titles: Prince of Hanover, Duke of
    Brunswick-Lüneburg, Prince of Great
    Britain and Ireland
Father: H.R.H. Ernst August, The Prince of
Hanover
Mother: H.H. Princess Ortrud of Schleswig-Holstein-Sonderburg-
    Glücksburg
Succeeded as Head of the Royal House of Hanover: 9 Dec 1987
Married (1): 30 Aug 1981 Marienburg, Germany (divorced 1997)
First wife: Chantal Hochuli
Children (by his 1st wife):
H.R.H. Prince Ernst August of Hanover (b.1983)
H.R.H. Prince Christian Heinrich of Hanover (b.1985)

The Prince of Hanover also carries British royal titles because he is
a direct male line descendant of King George III of Great Britain

who was also King of Hanover. The Thrones split when Victoria became Queen of Great Britain; women were not allowed to succeed to Hanover, so that throne when to Victoria's uncle, Prince Ernst August, Duke of Cumberland.

H.S.H. Princess Stephanie of Monaco
Sister of the Sovereign Prince
Born: 1 Feb 1965 Monaco
Full names: Stephanie Marie Elisabeth
Father: H.S.H. Rainier III, Prince of Monaco
Mother: Grace Kelly
Married (1): 1 Jul 1995 Monaco (divorced 1996)
First husband: Daniel Ducruet
Married (2): 12 Sep 2003 Vandoeuvres, Switzerland (divorced 2004)
Second husband: Adans Lopez Peres
Children:
by 1st husband:
Louis Ducruet (b.1992)
Pauline Ducruet (b.1994)
illegitimate by an undisclosed father:
Camille Gottlieb (b.1998)

Andrea Casiraghi
Nephew of the Sovereign Prince
Born: 8 Jun 1984 Monte Carlo, Monaco
Full names: Andrea Albert Pierre
Father: Stefano Casiraghi
Mother: H.S.H. Princess Caroline of Monaco

Although they have no titles, the children of Princess Caroline and Stefano Casiraghi are 2nd, 3rd, and 4th in line to the Princely Throne behind their mother.

Pierre Casiraghi
Nephew of the Sovereign Prince
Born: 5 Sep 1987 Monte Carlo, Monaco
Full names: Pierre Rainier Stefano
Father: Stefano Casiraghi
Mother: H.S.H. Princess Caroline of Monaco

Charlotte Casiraghi
Niece of the Sovereign Prince
Born: 3 Aug 1986 Monte Carlo, Monaco
Full names: Charlotte Marie Pomeline
Father: Stefano Casiraghi
Mother: H.S.H. Princess Caroline of Monaco

Photo Credits:
All photos in this sections are from the author's collection.

Netherlands

Current Sovereign: H.M. Beatrix, Queen of the Netherlands

Quick Life facts:
Born: 31 Jan 1938 Soestdijk Palace, Soest
Full names: Beatrix Wilhelmina Armgard
Full titles: Queen of the Netherlands, Princess of Orange-Nassau, Princess of Lippe-Biesterfeld, Marquise van Veere en Vlissingen, Countess van Buren, Culemborg, en Leerdam, von Dietz, Katzenelnbogen, und Spiegelberg, et de Vianden, Viscountess van Antwerp, Baroness van Breda, Cranendonk, Lands of Cujik, Eindhoven, City of Grave, Ijesselstein, en Liesveld, Diest, Herstal, en Warneton, von Beilstein, d'Arlay et Nozeroy, Hereditary Lady and Dame van Ameland, Lady von Baarn, Borculo, Bredevoort, Geertruidenberg, Hooge en Lage Zwaluwe, Klundert, Lichtenvoorde, 't Loo, Naaldwijk, Niervaart, Polanen, Steenbergen, Sint Maartensdijk, Soest, Ter Eem, Willemstad, en Zevenbergen, Bütgenbach, Sankt Vith, en Turnhout, de Besançon et Montfort, und Daasburg
Father: H.S.H. Prince Bernhard of Lippe-Biesterfeld
Mother: H.M. Queen Juliana of the Netherlands
Ascended Throne: 30 Apr 1980
Married: 10 Mar 1966 Amsterdam

Husband: Claus van Amsberg (d.2002)
Children:
H.R.H. The Prince of Orange (b.1967)
H.R.H. Prince Johan Frisco of Orange-Nassau (b.1968)
H.R.H. Prince Constantijn of the Netherlands (b.1969)
History of titles:
31 Jan 1938 - 30 Apr 1980; H.R.H. Princess Beatrix of the
    Netherlands
30 Apr 1980 - present: H.M. The Queen of the Netherlands

The Dutch monarchy in a nutshell:
For much of its history, the Netherlands has been a region under
the control of other powers. Early on, it fell into the hands of
Burgundy and went with it to the Habsburg empire when Emperor
Maximilian married the Burgundian heiress. After winning
independence from the Spanish Habsburgs in 1581, the Dutch
people establish a republic which lasts until 1795, under the elected
leadership of the Princes of Orange.

From 1795 to 1815, the Netherlands were controlled by the French
Empire of Napoleon. When the Congress of Vienna sorted out
Europe after Napoleonic domination, the Netherlands became a
separate kingdom encompassing the present day states of Belgium
and Luxembourg as well. Belgium gained their independence in
1830 and Luxembourg, already considered a separate country
under the same Crown, separated when a female, Wilhelmina,
inherited the Throne of the Netherlands. (See Luxembourg for the
rest of their story).

When the Kingdom was first established, they returned to the
Republican "Stadtholders" and selected the Prince of Orange to
become King. He took the name Willem I and was followed by
two more Willems until Willem III died in 1890 with no sons. He
was succeeded by his only surviving child, the 10-year old
Wilhelmina.

Wilhelmina was the first in a line of three reigning queens. She
was succeeded by her only child, Juliana, who was herself
succeeded by the eldest of her four daughters, Beatrix.

Abdication has become commonplace in the Netherlands. Of the six monarchs it has had, four have abdicated when they reached an elder age. With Queen Beatrix now 73, questions have started to come up about how long it will be before she follows suit.

Name of the Royal House:
Through all of the queens, the name of the House has remained that of Orange. Each generation has taken something of their paternal ancestry into account with their secondary titles. Queen Wilhelmina's husband was a Duke of Mecklenburg, a title that was carried by Queen Juliana. Juliana's husband was Prince Bernhard of Lippe-Biesterfeld. This too is a secondary title of each of his daughters. Queen Beatrix's husband was Claus van Amsberg, whose name is also reflected in the full titles of their children and grandchildren.

Titles within the Royal Family:
The basic titles are Prince or Princess of the Netherlands, Prince or Princess of Orange-Nassau with the predicate Royal Highness. Due to the constant changing of titles via female succession as well as the issue of consent for royal marriages, each person's titles are now somewhat on a case-by-case basis and will be explained in each person's profile. One consistency has been the husbands of the Queens. Each one has been granted the title Prince of the Netherlands upon their marriages with the predicate Royal Highness.

The heir-apparent automatically is titled Prince of Orange upon becoming the heir-apparent. His wife is not automatically titled Princess. As each prince is married, the Queen issues a decree as to how the wife will be styled. The usual case is to allow the wife to keep her own name. So the wife of the Prince of Orange is styled Princess Maxima of the Netherlands, not as the Princess of Orange.

Succession:
The succession law currently in place is from 1922 and limits the succession to three degrees of kinship from the current Sovereign. In the current situation, this limits the succession to the

descendants of the Queen, her sisters and their children. Grandchildren of the sisters are excluded because they are of the 4th degree of kinship from Beatrix. Two of the sisters, Irene and Cristina renounced their succession rights when they married Catholics. While this is not an automatic bar from succeeding as it is in Britain, renunciation was considered the correct move, politically.

Since 1983, the succession also follows the rules of gender-blind primogeniture. This means the Sovereign's eldest child will succeed regardless of gender.

There is also a marriage law to consider. Members of the royal family are required to seek consent from the government to marry. If they marry without such consent, they forfeit their place as a member of the Royal Family and their succession rights for themselves and their descendants. For this reason, the Queen's second son, Prince Johan Frisco is no longer considered a member of the Royal Family. The same is true for the Queen's nephews, Princes Pieter-Christiaan and Floris

Line of Succession:
1. H.R.H. The Prince of Orange
2. H.R.H. Princess Catharina-Amelia of the Netherlands
3. H.R.H. Princess Alexia of the Netherlands
4. H.R.H. Princess Ariane of the Netherlands
5. H.R.H. Prince Constantijn of the Netherlands
6. Countess Eloise of Orange-Nassau
7. Count Claus-Casimir of Orange-Nassau
8. Countess Leonore of Orange-Nassau
9. H.R.H. Princess Margriet of the Netherlands
10. H.H. Prince Maurits of Orange-Nassau
11. H.H. Prince Bernhard of Orange-Nassau

Under the degree of kinship rule, when the Prince of Orange succeeds the Throne, Princess Margriet will remain in succession but her children will fall off. By the same rule, if Margriet were to somehow come to the Throne, her grandchildren would then be added to the list.

Members of the Royal Family

H.R.H. The Prince of Orange
Son and heir-apparent to the Queen
Born: 27 Apr 1967 Utrecht, Netherlands
Full names: Willem-Alexander Claus
    George Ferdinand
Full titles: Prince of Orange, Prince of the
    Netherlands, Prince of Orange-Nassau,
    Jonkheer van Amsberg
Father: Claus van Amsberg
Mother: H.M. The Queen of the Netherlands
Married: 2 Feb 2002 Amsterdam
Wife: Máxima Zorreguieta Cerruti
Children:
H.R.H. Princess Catharina-Amelia of the Netherlands (b.2003)
H.R.H. Princess Alexia of the Netherlands (b.2005)
H.R.H. Princess Ariane of the Netherlands (b.2007)
History of titles:
27 Apr 1967 - 30 Apr 1980: H.R.H. Prince Willem-Alexander of
    the Netherlands
30 Apr 1980 - present: H.R.H. The Prince of Orange

The children of the Prince of Orange are fully titled Princess of the
Netherlands, Princess of Orange-Nassau

H.R.H. Princess Máxima of the Netherlands
Daughter-in-law of the Queen
Born: 17 May 1971 Buenos Aires,
    Argentina
Full names: Máxima
Father: Jorge Horacio Zorreguieta Stefanini
Mother: Maria del Carmen Cerruti Carricart
History of titles:
17 May 1971 - 2 Feb 2002: Miss Máxima
    Zorreguieta Cerruti
2 Feb 2002 - present: H.R.H. Princess Máxima of the Netherlands

Similar to Belgium, Máxima does not share her husband's title, Prince of Orange.

H.R.H. Princess Catharina-Amalia of the Netherlands
Granddaughter of the Queen
Born: 7 Dec 2003, The Hague
Full names: Catharina-Amalia Beatrix
     Carmen Victoria
Full titles: Princess of the Netherlands,
     Princess of Orange-Nassau
Father: H.R.H. The Prince of Orange
Mother: Máxima Zorreguieta Cerruti

H.R.H. Prince Constantijn of the Netherlands
Son of the Queen
Born: 11 Oct 1969 Utrecht, Netherlands
Full names: Constantijn Christof Frederik
     Aschwin
Full titles: Prince of the Netherlands, Prince
     of Orange-Nassau, Jonkheer van
     Amsberg
Father: Claus van Amsberg
Mother: H.M. The Queen of the
Netherlands
Married: 19 May 2001 The Hague, Netherlands
Wife: Laurentien Brinkhorst
Children:
Countess Eloise of Orange-Nassau (b.2002)
Count Claus-Casimir of Orange-Nassau (b.2004)
Countess Leonore of Orange-Nassau (b.2006)

Prince Constanijn's children are fully titled Count or Countess of Orange-Nassau, Jonkheer or Jonkvrouw van Amsberg

H.R.H. Princess Laurentien of the Netherlands
Daughter-in-law of the Queen
Born: 25 May 1966 Leiden, Netherlands
Full names: Petra Laurentien
Full titles: Princess of the Netherlands,
    Princess of Orange-Nassau, Jonkvrouw
    van Amsberg
Father: Laurens Jan Brinkhorst
Mother: Jantien Heringa
History of titles:
25 May 1966 - 19 May 2001: Miss Laurentien Brinkhorst
19 May 2001 - present: H.R.H. Princess Laurentien of the
    Netherlands

H.R.H. Princess Margriet of the Netherlands
Sister of the Queen
Born: 19 Jan 1943 Ottawa, Canada
Full names: Margriet Francisca
Full titles: Princess of the Netherlands,
    Princess of Orange-Nassau, Princess of
    Lippe-Biesterfeld
Father: H.S.H. Prince Bernhard of Lippe-
    Biesterfeld
Mother: H.M. Queen Juliana of the Netherlands
Married: 10 Jan 1967 The Hague, Netherlands
Husband: Pieter van Vollenhoven
Children:
H.H. Prince Maurits of Orange-Nassau (b.1968)
H.H. Prince Bernhard of Orange-Nassau (b.1969)
H.H. Prince Pieter-Christiaan of Orange-Nassau (b.1972)
H.H. Prince Floris of Orange-Nassau (b.1975)

H.H. Prince Maurits of Orange-Nassau
Nephew of the Queen
Born: 17 Apr 1968 Utrecht, Netherlands
Full names: Maurits Willem Pieter Hendrik
Full titles: Prince of Orange-Nassau, van
    Vollenhoven
Father: Pieter van Vollenhoven
Mother: H.R.H. Princess Margriet of the
    Netherlands
Married: 30 May 1998 Apeldoorn,
    Netherlands
Wife: Marilène van den Broek
Children:
Anastasia van Lippe-Biesterfeld van Vollenhoven (b.2001)
Lucas van Lippe-Biesterfeld van Vollenhoven (b.2002)
Felicia van Lippe-Biesterfeld van Vollenhoven (b.2005)

The children of Prince Maurits have no titles, only the surname
"van Lippe-Biesterfeld van Vollenhoven". His wife is titled
Princess Marilène of Orange-Nassau, van Vollenhoven-van den
Broek

H.H. Prince Bernhard of Orange-Nassau
Nephew of the Queen
Born: 25 Dec 1969 Utrecht, Netherlands
Full names: Bernhard Lucas Emanuel
Full titles: Prince of Orange-Nassau, van
    Vollenhoven
Father: Pieter van Vollenhoven
Mother: H.R.H. Princess Margriet of the
    Netherlands
Married: 8 Jul 2000 Utrecht, Netherlands
Wife: Annette Sekrève
Children:
Isabella van Vollenhoven (b.2002)
Samuel van Vollenhoven (b.2004)
Benjamin van Vollenhoven (b.2008)

The children of Prince Bernhard have no title, only the surname van Vollenhoven. His wife is titled Princess of Orange-Nassau, van Vollenhoven-Sekrève

Other Members of the Queen's Family

H.R.H. Prince Frisco of Orange-Nassau (b.1968) Son of the Queen. He lost his place in the Royal Family when he married, without governmental consent, Mabel Wisse Smit, now **Princess Mabel of Orange-Nassau**. Their children are titles Count or Countess of Orange-Nassau, Jonkheer or Jonkvrouw van Amsberg. Their children are **Countess Emma** (b.2005) and **Countess Joanna** (b.2006)

H.H. Prince Pieter-Christaan of Orange-Nassau (b.1972) Nephew of the Queen, son of Princess Margriet. He lost his place in the Royal Family when he married, without governmental consent, Anita van Eijk, now **Princess Anita of Orange-Nassau**. Their children have no titles and are simply surnamed van Vollenhoven. Their children are **Emma** (b.2006) and **Pieter** (b.2008)

H.H. Prince Floris of Orange-Nassau (b.1975) Nephew of the Queen, son of Princess Margriet. He lost his place in the Royal Family when he married, without governmental consent, Aimée Söhngren, now **Princess Aimée of Orange-Nassau**. Their children have no titles and are simply surnamed van Vollenhoven. Their children are **Magali** (b.2007) and **Eliane** (b.2009).

H.R.H. Princess Irene of the Netherlands (b.1939) Sister of the Queen. She lost his place in the Royal Family when he married, without governmental consent, Prince Carlos Hugo of Bourbon-Parma, after 1977, **The Duke of Parma**, who died in 2010. Her marriage created quite an uproar due to the acrimonious history between the Netherlands and Spain. The Duke was the Carlist claimant to the Spanish Throne. After her marriage she was obliged to live outside of the Netherlands. She was able to return after her 1981 divorce. Her children received no titles from her, but from their father they are titled Prince or Princess of Bourbon-

Parma and the elder son succeeded his father as the Duke of Parma in 2010. Princess Irene's children are **Carlos Javier, Duke of Parma** (b.1970), **Princess Margarita** (b.1972), **Prince Jaime** (b.1972 - twin with Margarita), and **Princess Maria Carolina** (b.1974).

H.R.H. Princess Christina of the Netherlands (b.1947) Sister of the Queen. When she chose to marry a Roman Catholic, **Jorge Guillermo,** in 1975, (they divorced in 1996), she renounced her succession rights for herself and her descendants. Their children have no titles and are surnamed Guillermo: **Bernardo** (b.1977), **Nicolás** (b.1979), and **Juliana** (b.1981).

Photo Credits:
Photos of the Queen and Princess Margriet are from the author's collection. The rest of the photos are courtesy the press office of the Royal House.

Norway

Current Sovereign: H.M. Harald V, King of Norway

Quick Life Facts:
Born: 21 Feb 1937 Skaugum, Norway
Full names: Harald
Full titles: King of Norway
Father: H.M. Olav V, King of Norway
Mother: H.R.H. Princess Märtha of Sweden
Ascended Throne: 17 Jan 1991
Royal Oath Sworn: 21 Jan 1991
Married: 26 Aug 1968 Oslo
Wife: Sonja Haraldsen
Children:
H.H. Princess Märtha Louise of Norway (b.1971)
H.R.H. Crown Prince Haakon of Norway (b.1973)
History of titles:
21 Feb 1937 - 21 Sep 1957: H.R.H. Prince Harald of Norway
21 Sep 1957 - 17 Jan 1991: H.R.H. Crown Prince Harold of
    Norway
17 Jan 1991 - present: H.M. The King of Norway

Norwegian monarchy in a nutshell:

The present royal house has a short history, only since 1905. Prior to that Norway spent over 500 years as either a province of Denmark or of Sweden. The last of the old Norse kings died in 1388. When a new independent Kingdom of Norway was established in 1905, the kings continued the numbering used by the kings of old.

Norway was peacefully granted independence from Sweden by referendum, and the Norwegian parliament, The Storting, elected Prince Carl of Denmark to be their new King. Prince Carl was the second son of the then-Crown Prince of Denmark, later King Frederik VIII. Upon his ascension to the Norwegian Throne, he took the name Haakon VII as their King.

King Haakon was married to the youngest daughter of Britain's King Edward VII, making Norway's Royal Family the most closely related by blood to Britain's current Queen. Queen Elizabeth and King Harald are 2nd cousins. Through their mother, The King and his sisters are 1st cousins to the late King Baudouin and King Albert II of the Belgians, and the late Grand Duchess Josephine-Charlotte of Luxembourg

The father of the current King, Olav V reigned from 1957 until his death in 1991. He was the last living grandchild of Britain's King Edward VII. His wife, Princess Märtha of Sweden, died in 1954 while still Crown Princess, so was never queen.

Today, the Norwegian Royal Family is famous for its closeness to their subjects, and for being generally less formal than many of their counterparts in other countries.

Titles in the Royal Family:
Members of the Royal Family are titled Prince or Princess of Norway. The heir- or heiress-apparent is styled Crown Prince or Crown Princess of Norway. Prior to 2002, all members of the Royal Family were styled His or Her Royal Highness. In 2002, this was restricted to the heir-apparent and their eldest child, the rest of the family members being styled His or Her Highness.

The House Name of the Royal Family:
Like their ancestors, the Kings of Denmark, the Norwegian Royal Family does not have a surname. They are of the House of Schleswig-Holstein-Sonderburg-Glücksburg, as are the royal families of Denmark and Greece.

Succession:
In 1990 the succession laws were changed from being an all-male succession to being a gender-blind succession, however for people born prior to 1990, males would take precedence over females among siblings. This last line only affects Crown Prince Haakon and his sister, Princess Märtha Louise as they were, at that time, the only people with succession right where a sister was older than a brother.
Succession:
1. H.R.H. Crown Prince Haakon of Norway
2. H.R.H. Princess Ingrid of Norway
3. H.H. Prince Sverre of Norway
4. H.H. Princess Märtha Louise of Norway
5. Maud Behn
6. Leah Behn
7. Emma Behn

Members of the Royal Family

H.M. The Queen of Norway
Wife of the King
Born: 4 Jul 1937 Oslo
Full Names: Sonja
Father: Karl August Haraldsen
Mother: Dagny Ulrichsen
History of titles:
4 Jul 1937 - 29 Aug 1968: Miss Sonja
    Haraldsen
29 Aug 1968 - 17 Jan 1991: H.R.H.
Crown Princess Sonja of Norway
17 Jan 1991 - present: H.M. The Queen

H.R.H. Crown Prince Haakon of Norway
Son and Heir-apparent of the King
Born: 20 Jul 1973 Oslo
Full names: Haakon Magnus
Father: H.M. The King of Norway
Mother: Sonja Haraldsen
Married: 25 Aug 2001 Oslo
Wife: Mette-Marit Høiby
Children:
H.R.H. Princess Ingrid (b.2004)
H.H. Prince Sverre (b.2005)
History of titles:
20 Jul 1973 - 17 Jan 1991: H.R.H. Prince Haakon of Norway
17 Jan 1991 - present: H.R.H. Crown Prince Haakon of Norway

H.R.H. Crown Princess Mette-Marit of Norway
Daughter-in-law of the King
Born: 19 Aug 1973 Kristiansaand,
    Norway
Full names: Mette-Marit Tjessem
Father: Sven Høiby
Mother: Marit Tjessem
Additional children:
by Morten Borg:
Marius Høiby (b.1997)
History of titles:
19 Aug 1973 - 25 Aug 2001: Miss Mette-Marit Høiby
25 Aug 2001 - present: H.R.H. Crown Princess Mette-Marit of
    Norway

H.R.H. Princess Ingrid of Norway
Granddaughter of the King
Born: 21 Jan 2004 Oslo
Full names: Ingrid Alexandra
Father: H.R.H. Crown Prince Haakon of
Norway
Mother: Matte-Marit Tjessem

H.H. Princess Märtha Louise of Norway
Daughter of the King
Born: 22 Sep 1971 Oslo
Full names: Märtha Louise
Father: H.M. The King of Norway
Mother: Sonja Haraldsen
Married: 24 May 2002 Trondheim,
    Norway
Husband: Ari Behn
Children:
Maud Behn (b.2003)
Leah Behn (b.2005)
Emma Behn (b.2008)
History of titles:
22 Sep 1971 - 24 May 2002: H.R.H. Princess Märtha Louise of
    Norway
24 May 2002 - present: H.H. Princess Märtha Louise of Norway

H.H. Princess Ragnhild, Mrs. Lorentzen
Sister of the King
Born: 9 Jun 1930
Full names: Ragnhild Alexandra
Father: H.M. King Olav V of Norway
Mother: H.R.H. Princess Märtha of
    Sweden
Married: 15 May 1953 Asker, Norway
Husband: Erling Lorentzen

Children:
Haakon Lorentzen (b.1954)
Ingeborg Ribeiro (b.1957)
Ragnhild Long (b.1968)
History of titles:
9 Jun 1930 - 15 May 1953: H.R.H. Princess Ragnhild of Norway
15 May 1953 - 24 May 2002: Princess Ragnhild, Mrs. Lorentzen
24 May 2002 - present: H.H. Princess Ragnhild, Mrs. Lorentzen

Upon her marriage to a commoner she was deprived of the style
Royal Highness until 2002 when, after the marriage of both
children of the King to commoners, she was granted the style
Highness

H.H. Princess Astrid, Mrs. Ferner
Sister of the King
Born: 12 Feb 1932 Oslo
Full names: Astrid Maud Ingeborg
Father: H.M. King Olav V of Norway
Mother: H.R.H. Princess Märtha of
     Sweden
Married: 12 Jan 1961 Asker, Norway
Husband: Johan Ferner
Children:
Catherine Johansen (b.1962)
Benedikte Ferner (b.1963)
Alexander Ferner (b.1965)
Elisabeth Beckman (b.1969)
Carl-Christian Ferner (b.1972)
History of titles:
12 Feb 1932 - 12 Jan 1961: H.R.H. Princess Astrid of Norway
12 Jan 1961 - 24 May 2002: Princess Astrid, Mrs. Ferner
24 May 2002 - present: H.H. Princess Astrid, Mrs. Ferner

Photo Credits: All photos are courtesy of the Royal House of
Norway.

Spain

Current Sovereign: His Majesty, Juan Carlos, King of Spain

Quick Life Facts:
Born: 5 Jan 1938 Rome, Italy
Full names: Juan Carlos Alfonso Victor Maria
Full titles: King of Spain, of Castile, of León, of Aragon, of the
Two Sicilies, of Jerusalem, of Navarre, of Granada, of Toledo,
of Valencia, of Galicia, of Majorca, of Seville, of Sardinia, of
Córdoba, of Corsica, of Murcia, of Menorca, of Jaén, of the
Algarves, of Algeciras, of Gibraltar, of the Canary Islands, of
the Spanish East and West Indies, and of the Islands and
Mainland of the Ocean Sea, Archduke of Austria, Duke of
Burgundy, of Brabant, of Milan, and of Neopatra, Count of
Habsburg, of Flanders, of Tyrol, of Roussillon, and of
Barcelona, Lord of Biscay and of Molina.
Father: H.R.H. Infante Juan of Spain, Count of Barcelona
Mother: H.R.H. Princess Maria de las Mercedes of the Two
Sicilies
Ascended Throne: 22 Nov 1975
Anointed as King: 27 Nov 1975
Married: 14 May 1962 Athens, Greece
Wife: H.R.H. Princess Sophie of Greece
Children:

H.R.H. The Duchess of Lugo (b.1963)
H.R.H. The Duchess of Palma de Mallorca (b.1965)
H.R.H. The Prince of Asturias (b.1968)
History of titles:
5 Jan 1938 - 15 Jan 1941: H.R.H. Infante Juan Carlos of Spain
15 Jan 1941 - 22 Nov 1975: H.R.H. The Prince of Asturias*
22 Nov 1975 - present: H.M. The King of Spain

*From 1969-1975, Gen. Franco titled Juan Carlos as the Prince of
Spain, a title generally not used by the monarchy.

Spanish monarchy in a nutshell:
The Iberian peninsula was divided into several small kingdoms,
some of which were conquered and controlled by Muslims (called
the Moorish Kingdoms) for several centuries. The two most
prominent kingdoms to emerge were Aragon and Castile. They
were united by the marriage of King Ferdinand II of Aragon and
Queen Isabella I of Castile in 1469. In 1492, their combined forces
were able to liberate the last of the Iberian lands from Muslim
control.

Ferdinand and Isabella did not have surviving sons so their heiress
was their mentally disturbed daughter, Juana, who was married to
Archduke Philip of Austria. Juana's entire reign was under the
Regency of her husband, and later their son. Philip and Juana's
descendants continued to rule until 1700, covering the period of
Spain's greatest ascension as a world power.

The death of the last Spanish Habsburg in 1700 prompted the War
of Spanish Succession between Austria, who claimed the Throne
by being the next male heir, and France, who was most closely
related through female lines. France won, but the Treaty that ended
the war stipulated France and Spain could not be joined under the
same Crown, so the Spanish Throne went to a grandson of the
French King, Philippe, Duke of Anjou, who took the Spanish
Throne as King Felipe V. His descendants have ruled Spain ever
since, except during the Napoleonic era and during the Franco
regime in the 20th century.

A communist uprising forced King Alfonso XIII to flee the country in 1931. Francisco Franco and his nationalist forces won the following Spanish Civil War, but did not want Alfonso as King forcing him to abdicate in 1941. Franco was set up as a virtual dictator and held control until his death in 1975. Franco had always considered Spain to have remained a monarchy with him acting as Curator of the Throne. Towards the end of his life he selected Prince Juan Carlos, grandson of Alfonso XIII, to be his successor. Juan Carlos became King upon Franco's death . He was shortly thereafter recognized by his father, Don Juan, who was the rightful King according to Alfonso's abdication.

The Name of the Royal Family:
Since 1700, the Royal Family of Spain has been the House and Family of Bourbon (Borbón in Spanish). Extended family of the King who are no longer royal carry de Borbón as their surname. It is Spanish tradition that a person's surname is their father's surname followed by their mother's surname with the Spanish word for 'and' (y) connecting them. For example, both of the King's parents are from the House of Bourbon, so his surname, if he used it, would be de Borbón y Borbón.

Titles within the Royal Family:
The standard title for royal family members is Infante or Infanta (plural = Infantos) of Spain with the predicate Royal Highness. The heir to the Throne, whether it be an heir-apparent or an heir-presumptive, is styled Prince or Princess of Asturias. This title is not automatic since 1978, it has to be created for the heir. When a person is created Prince (or Princess) of Asturias, it replaces the title Infante/Infanta of Spain

The title Infante is limited to the children of the Sovereign and the children of the Prince of Asturias. However, historically, the title has been extended to several other family members on a case-by-case basis. Currently the only Infantos are the King's children, the Prince of Asturias's children, the King's sisters, and one cousin.

The children of the King's daughters have been granted the predicate His or Her Excellency and have been created Grandees of Spain, a title unique to Spain which had far more power and meaning in previous centuries.

The King may also bestow titles of nobility upon his relatives. The recent trend has been to do this upon the marriage of the person involved. Spanish noble titles do not follow a set of automatic succession rules. Each holder of a title must appoint an heir, if they do not, potential heirs must petition the Crown for the title to be passed to them. It is common practice for members of the nobility, who often hold multiple titles, to cede their titles to their designated heirs while they are still alive. It is also common practice to divide multiple titles amongst their children.

All members of Spanish nobility and royalty also have the style Don or Doña before their names. Typically, English translation leaves this style off for the Infantos and the Kings and Queens.

In the past, the King of Spain used the style His Catholic Majesty which was granted by the Pope to King Ferdinand and Queen Isabella. When the monarchy was restored in 1975, King Juan Carlos chose not to use this style.

Succession:
The current Succession Law limits the succession to the "heirs" of King Juan Carlos, but this ambiguous term does not necessarily mean only his descendants. As the King currently has eight grandchildren, it does not seem likely a need for more clarification will be needed.

Succession follows the lines of male-preference primogeniture. This means male children have precedence over female children within the same family.

Line of Succession:
1. H.R.H. The Prince of the Asturias
2. H.R.H. Infanta Leonor of Spain
3. H.R.H. Infanta Sofia of Spain
4. H.R.H. The Duchess of Lugo
5. Don Juan Frolián de Marichalar y Borbón

6. Doña Victoria de Marichalar y Borbón
7. H.R.H. The Duchess of Palma de Majorca
8. Don Juan Urdangarin y de Borbón
9. Don Pablo Urdangarin y de Borbón
10. Don Miguel Urdangarin y de Borbón
11. Doña Irene Urdangarin y de Borbón

Members of the Royal Family

H.M. The Queen of Spain
Wife of the King
Born: 2 Nov 1938 Psychiko, Greece
Full name: Sofia
Full titles: Queen of Spain, etc, Princess of
    Greece and Denmark
Father: H.M. Paul, King of the Hellenes
Mother: H.R.H. Princess Frederika of
    Hanover
History of titles:
    2 Nov 1938 - 14 May 1962: H.R.H.
Princess Sofia of Greece
14 May 1962 - 22 Nov 1975: H.R.H. The Princess of Asturias
22 Nov 1975 - present: H.M. The Queen of Spain

H.R.H. The Prince of Asturias
Son and heir-apparent of the King
Born: 30 Jan 1968 Madrid
Full names: Felipe Juan Pablo Alfonso y
    Todos los Santos
Full titles: Prince of Asturias, Prince of
    Viana, Prince of Girona, Duke of
    Montblanc, Count de Cervera, Lord de
    Balaguer
Father: H.M. The King of Spain
Mother: H.R.H. Princess Sofia of Greece
Married: 22 May 2004 Madrid
Wife: Letizia Ortiz Rocasolano
Children:
H.R.H. Infanta Leonor of Spain (b.2005)

H.R.H. Infanta Sofia of Spain (b.2007)
History of titles:
30 Jan 1968 - 22 Jan 1977: H.R.H. Infante Felipe of Spain
22 Jan 1977 - present: H.R.H. The Prince of Asturias

If the Prince and Princess of Asturias have no sons, Leonor will be the future Queen of Spain.

H.R.H. The Princess of Asturias
Daughter-in-law of the King
Born: 15 Sep 1972 Oviedo, Spain
Full names: Letizia
Father: Jesús José Ortiz Álvarez
Mother: Maria de la Paloma Rocasolano
    Rodríguez
Married (1): 7 Aug 1998 Almendarlejo,
    Spain (divorced 1999)
First husband: Alonso Guerrero Pérez (no
    issue)
History of titles:
15 Sep 1972 - 22 May 2004: Letizia Ortiz Rocasolano
22 May 2004 - present: H.R.H. The Princess of the Asturias

Letizia's first marriage was civil only so no annulment was needed for her to marry Prince Felipe.

H.R.H. Infanta Leonor of Spain
Granddaughter of the King
Born: 31 Oct 2005 Madrid
Full names: Leonor
Father: H.R.H. The Prince of Asturias
Mother: Letizia Ortiz Rocasolano

If the Prince and Princess of Asturias have no sons, Leonor will one day be Queen of Spain.

H.R.H. The Duchess of Lugo
Daughter of the King
Born: 20 Dec 1963 Madrid
Full names: Elena Maria Isabel Dominica
Full titles: Infanta of Spain, Duchess of
   Lugo
Father: H.M. The King of Spain
Mother: H.R.H. Princess Sofia of Greece
Married: 18 Mar 1995 Seville, Spain
   (divorced 2010)
Former Husband: Jaime de Marichalar y
Sáenz de Téjada
Children:
Don Felipe de Marichalar y Borbón (b.1998)
Doña Victoria de Marichalar y Borbón (b.2000)
History of titles:
20 Dec 1963 - 18 Mar 1995: H.R.H. Infanta Elena of Spain
18 Mar 1995 - present: H.R.H. The Duchess of Lugo

During the marriage, Jaime was also styled Duke of Lugo, but is
not permitted to use the style since the divorce. Little Don Felipe is
often called Frolián (his 3rd name) in the press, but the family calls
him Felipe.

**H.R.H. The Duchess of Palma de
Mallorca**
Daughter of the King
Born: 13 Jun 1965 Madrid
Full names: Cristina Frederica Victoria
   Antonia de la Santísima Trinidad
Full titles: Infanta of Spain, Duchess of
   Palma de Mallorca
Father: H.M. The King of Spain
Mother: H.R.H. Princess Sofia of Greece
Married: 4 Oct 1997 Barcelona, Spain
Husband: Iñaki Urdangarin (titular Duke
   of Palma de Mallorca)
Children:
Don Juan Urdangarin y de Borbón (b.1999)

Don Pablo Urdangarin y de Borbón (b.2000)
Don Miguel Urdangarin y de Borbón (b.2002)
Doña Irene Urdangarin y de Borbón (b.2005)
History of titles:
13 Jun 1965 - 4 Oct 1997: H.R.H. Infanta Cristina of Spain
4 Oct 1997 - present: H.R.H. The Duchess of Palma de Mallorca

By Spanish custom, the husband of a lady holding a title of
nobility may share that title. So Iñaki is also styled as the Duke of
Palma de Mallorca.

H.R.H. The Duchess of Badajoz
Sister of the King
Born: 30 Jul 1936 Cannes, France
Full names: Maria del Pilar Alfonsa Juana
    Vitoria Luisa y Todos los Santos
Full titles: Infanta of Spain, Duchess of
    Badajoz, Dowager Viscountess de la
    Torre
Father: H.R.H. The Count de Barcelona
Mother: H.R.H. Princess Maria de las
    Mercedes of the Two Sicilies
Married: 6 May 1967 Lisbon, Portugal
Husband: Luis Gómez-Acebo y de Estrada, Viscount de la Torre
    (d.1991)
Children:
Doña Simonetta Gómez-Acebo y de Borbón (b.1968)
Don Juan Gómez-Acebo y de Borbón, Viscount de la Torre
    (b.1969)
Don Bruno Gómez-Acebo y de Borbón (b.1971)
Don Beltrán Gómez-Acebo y de Borbón (b.1973)
Don Fernando Gómez-Acebo y de Borbón (b.1974)
History of titles:
30 Jul 1936 - 6 May 1967: H.R.H. Infanta Pilar of Spain
6 May 1967 - 23 Jun 1981: H.R.H. The Viscountess de la Torre
23 Jun 1981 - present: H.R.H. The Duchess of Badajoz

H.R.H. The Duchess of Soria and Hernani
Sister of the King
Born: 6 Mar 1939 Rome, Italy
Full names: Margarita Maria de la
    Victoria Esperanza Jacoba
    Felicidad Perpetua y Todos los
    Santos
Full titles: Infanta of Spain, 2nd Duchess of
Hernani, Duchess of Soria
Father: H.R.H. The Count de Barcelona
Mother: H.R.H. Princess Maria de las Mercedes of the Two
    Sicilies
Married: 12 Oct 1972 Estoril, Portugal
Husband: Carlos Zurita y Delgado, titular Duke of Soria
Children:
Don Alfonso Zurita y de Borbón (b.1973)
Doña Maria Sofia Zurita y de Borbón (b.1975)
History of titles:
6 Mar 1939 - 27 May 1981: H.R.H. Infanta Margarita of Spain
27 May 1981 - 23 Jun 1981: H.R.H. The Duchess of Hernani
23 Jun 1981 - present: H.R.H. The Duchess of Soria and Hernani

A distant cousin, Don Manfredo de Borbón willed his title Duke of Hernani to Margarita. She was created a few weeks later Duchess of Soria for life, a title she can share with her husband.

Other Members of the King's Family

Don Luis Alfonso de Borbón (b.1974) 1st cousin once removed of the King, great-grandson son of King Alfonso XIII. His grandfather Jaime, Duke of Segovia renounced his succession rights in Spain, but this line of the family has since become the senior most line of France (see France).

H.R.H. Infante Carlos, Duke of Calabria (b.1938) Maternal 1st cousin of the King. At one point his grandmother was heiress-presumptive to the Throne of Spain, until her brother, King

Alfonso XIII became a father. Infante Carlos is in a dispute over the headship of the Royal House of the Two Sicilies (see Italy)

Leandro Alfonso de Borbón y Ruíz-Moragas (b.1929) Uncle of the King. Illegitimate son of King Alfonso XIII and Maria del Carmen Ruíz y Moragas, an actress. Recognized by Judicial order to be King Alfonso's son in 2003. His six children have all also taken the name de Borbón.

There are also several male lines of the Bourbon family descended from King Felipe V. These include the Royal House of the Two Sicilies and the Ducal House of Parma (see Italy), the Grand Ducal House of Luxembourg (see Luxembourg), as well as the Spanish noble families of the Duke of Seville, the Marques de Squilache, and the Duke of Santa Elena.

Photo Credits:
All photos in this section are from the author's collection.

Sweden

Current Sovereign: His Majesty, Carl XVI Gustaf, King of Sweden

Quick Life Facts:
Born: 30 Apr 1946 Haga Palace, near Stockholm
Full names: Carl Gustaf Folke Hubertus
Full titles: King of Sweden, King of the Goths and the Wends
Father: H.R.H. Prince Gustaf Adolf, Duke of Västerbotten
Mother: H.H. Princess Sibylle of Saxe-Coburg and Gotha
Ascended Throne: 15 Sep 1973
Took Oath: 19 Sep 1973
Married: 19 Jun 1976 Stockholm
Wife: Silvia Sommerlath
Children:
H.R.H. Crown Princess Victoria, Duchess of Västergötland
    (b.1977)
H.R.H. Prince Carl Philip, Duke of Värmland (b.1979)
H.R.H. Princess Madeleine, Duchess of Hälsingland and
    Gästrikland (b.1982)
History of titles:
30 Apr - 7 Jun 1946: H.R.H. Hereditary Prince Carl Gustaf of

Sweden

7 Jun 1946 - 29 Oct 1950: H.R.H. Hereditary Prince Carl Gustaf, Duke of Jämtland

29 Oct 1950 - 15 Sep 1973: H.R.H. Crown Prince Carl Gustaf, Duke of Jämtland

15 Sep 1973 - present: H.M. The King of Sweden

The Swedish monarchy in a nutshell:

It is not really known when the kings of Sweden began, but most lists of Swedish Kings start with Erik the Victorious (d.995) as he was the first to rule over the Swedes and the Goths. His descendants continued rule through various House names until 1523.

The House of Vasa was elected to the Throne in the person of Gustaf I after the extinction of the previous dynasty and a period of Danish control. Gustaf had been instrumental in driving the Danes out. His descendants would continue until 1818, also passing through a few females into other Houses along the way.

In 1810, King Carl XIII, who was then old and heirless, adopted Marshal Jean-Baptiste Bernadotte, a Napoleonic military commander, to be his heir. The choice of heir was made by governmental officials who had become impressed with Bernadotte early in the Napoleonic Wars. Carl XIII died in 1818, was succeeded by Bernadotte as King Carl XIV Johan, and the Bernadottes have reigned ever since.

During the Napoleonic Wars, Sweden was able to wrest Norway away from Denmark and keep it under its own Crown until a referendum made it independent in 1905.

Today the Swedish royal family is a very compact family unit, but is about to expand with the recent marriage of the first of King Carl Gustaf's children.

The Family name of the Royal Family:

Since 1818 the House and Name of the Royal Family has been Bernadotte. It has already been announced that any children of

Crown Princess Victoria will retain both the House and Family name of Bernadotte.

Titles within the Royal Family
The basic title for family members is Prince or Princess of Sweden with the predicate His or Her Royal Highness. Members of the Royal Family who are in line of succession are all also given a Dukedom.

Marriages in the royal family must have the King's consent, and prior to the 1970's, this consent would only be given for marriages of a Prince to Princess of another reigning house. When a Prince married without consent, they automatically lost their title of Prince and assumed the surname Bernadotte. By 1951, several princes had entered such marriages. The Grand Duchess of Luxembourg extended to them all the title Count af Wisborg, a hereditary title their descendants continue to carry. During this period several Princesses also married commoners and were also deprived of their royal status. However, since they did not have succession rights to begin with, they were styled as Princess Firstname, Mrs. Husband's name.

When the King fell in love with Silvia Sommerlath, he decided to allow future marriages to commoners with royal consent. This has been applied twice so far: for his uncle, Prince Bertil, and his daughter, Crown Princess Victoria.

When Crown Princess Victoria married in 2010, her husband was created a Prince of Sweden and Duke of Västergötland with the predicate His Royal Highness.

Succession:
Succession was male-only until 1980 when the law was changed to not only allow female succession but also to allow the first born children to succeed regardless of gender. The new law also limited the succession to the descendants of the current King. Sweden was the first European country to adopt a gender-blind rule, but has since been followed by Norway, Denmark, Netherlands, and

Belgium. Luxembourg, Spain, and Great Britain also have similar rule changes currently under consideration.

Line of Succession:
1. H.R.H. Crown Princess Victoria, Duchess of Västergötland
2. H.R.H. Prince Carl Philip, Duke of Värmland
3. H.R.H. Princess Madeleine, Duchess of Hälsingborg and
    Gästrikland

Members of the Royal Family

H.M. The Queen of Sweden
Wife of the King
Born: 23 Dec 1943 Heidelberg, Germany
Full names: Silvia Renate
Father: Walther Sommerlath
Mother: Alice de Toledo
History of titles:
23 Dec 1943 - 19 Jun 1976: Miss Silvia
    Sommerlath
19 Jun 1976 - present: H.M. The Queen of
    Sweden

**H.R.H. Crown Princess Victoria,
Duchess of Västergötland**
Daughter and heiress-apparent to the King
Born: 14 Jul 1977 Stockholm
Full names: Victoria Ingrid Alice Désirée
Full titles: Crown Princess of Sweden,
    Duchess of Västergötland
Father: H.M. The King of the Sweden
Mother: Silvia Sommerlath
Married: 19 Jun 2010 Stockholm
Husband: Daniel Westling
Children: The Crown Princess expects her first child in March,
    2012.
History of titles:
14 Jul 1977 - 31 Dec 1979: H.R.H. Princess Victoria of Sweden

1 Jan 1980 - present: H.R.H. Crown Princess Victoria, Duchess of
Västergötland

H.R.H. Prince Daniel, Duke of
Västergötland
Son-in-law of the King
Born: 15 Sep 1973 Örebro, Sweden
Full names: Olof Daniel
Full titles: Prince of Sweden, Duke of
Västergötland
Father: Olle Gunnar
Mother: Eva Westling
History of titles:
15 Sep 1973 - 19 Jun 2010: Daniel
Westling
19 Jun 2010 - present: H.R.H. Prince
Daniel, Duke of Västergötland

H.R.H. Prince Carl Philip, Duke of
Värmland
Son of the King
Born: 13 May 1979 Stockholm
Full names: Carl Philip Edmund Bertil
Full titles: Prince of Sweden, Duke of
Värmland
Father: H.M. The King of Sweden
Mother: Silvia Sommerlath
History of titles:
13 May 1979 - 31 Dec 1979: H.R.H.
Crown Prince Carl Philip of Sweden
1 Jan 1980 - present: H.R.H. Prince Carl Philip, Duke of Värmland

H.R.H. Princess Madeleine, Duchess of Hälsingborg and Gästrikland
Daughter of the King
Born: 10 Jun 1982 Drottningholm, Sweden
Full names: Madeleine Thérèse Amélie
    Joséphine
Full titles: Princess of Sweden, Duchess of
    Hälsingborg and Gästrikland
Father: H.M. The King of Sweden
Mother: Silvia Sommerlath

Princess Madeline was engaged in August 2009 to Jonas Bergström but the engagement was called off the following April.

H.R.H. Princess Birgitta of Sweden
Sister of the King
Born: 19 Jan 1937 Haga Palace, near
    Stockholm
Full names: Birgitta Ingeborg Alice
Full titles: Princess of Sweden, Princess of
    Hohenzollern
Father: H.R.H. Prince Gustaf Adolf, Duke
    of Västerbotten
Mother: H.H. Princess Sibylle of Saxe-
    Coburg and Gotha
Married: 25 May 1961 Stockholm (civil) & 30 May 1961
    Sigmaringen, Germany (religious) (separated 1990)
Husband: H.S.H. Prince Johann Georg of Hohenzollern
Children:
H.S.H. Prince Carl Christian of Hohenzollern (b.1962)
H.S.H. Désirée von Bohlen und Halbach (b.1963)
H.S.H. Prince Hubertus of Hohenzollern (b.1966)

Princess Birgitta has been separated from her husband since 1990 but has not divorced. However, she chooses to be known as Princess of Sweden versus Princess of Hohenzollern.

H.R.H. Princess Lilian, Duchess of Halland
Aunt of the King, widow of Prince Bertil
Born: 30 Aug 1915 Swansea, England
Full names: Lilian May
Full titles: Princess of Sweden, Duchess
    of Halland
Father: William Davies
Mother: Gladys Curran
Married (1): 27 Sep 1940 Horsham, England (divorced 1947)
First husband: Ivan Craig (d.1994)
Married (2): 7 Dec 1976 Drottningholm Palace, Sweden
Second husband: H.R.H. Prince Bertil, Duke of Halland (d.1997)
No children
History of titles:
30 Aug 1915 - 27 Sep 1940: Lilian Davies
27 Sep 1940 - 7 Dec 1976: Mrs. Lilian Craig
7 Dec 1976 - present: H.R.H. Princess Lilian, Duchess of Halland

It was announced in June 2010 that Princess Lilian suffers from Alzheimer's syndrome and will no longer be able to participate in public events.

Other Members of the King's Family

Princess Margaretha, Mrs. Ambler (b.1934) Sister of the King. Lost royal prerogatives when she married a commoner, **John Amber** (d.2008). Their children are **Baroness Sibylle von Dincklage** (b.1965), **Charles Ambler** (b.1966), and **James Ambler** (b.1967)

Princess Désirée. Baroness Silfvershiold (b.1938) Sister of the King. Lost royal prerogatives when she married a commoner, **Baron Nils-August Silfverschiold**. Their children are **Baron Carl** (b.1965), **Baroness Kristina-Louisa de Geer af Finspång** (b.1963), and **Baroness Helene** (b.1968)

Princess Christina, Mrs. Magnuson (b.1943) Sister of the King. Lost royal prerogatives when she married a commoner, **Tord Magnuson**. Their children are **Gustaf** (b.1975), **Oscar** (b.1977), and **Victor** (b.1980)

Count Carl Johan Bernadotte af Wisborg (b.1916) Uncle of the King, son of King Gustaf VI. Lost royal prerogatives when he married a commoner. Created Count af Wisborg by the Grand Duchess of Luxemburg in 1951. He has been married twice and has two adopted children. He is also the last living great-grandchild of Queen Victoria of Great Britain. His maternal grandfather was the Queen's son, Prince Arthur, Duke Connaught.

Additionally there are several other more distant cousins who are styled Count af Wisborg.

Photo Credits:
All photos in this section are from the author's collection.

Former Reigning Royal Families

Albania:

The Albanian Royal Family began with Zog I, who was declared King 1928, having previously been serving as President. The Kingdom only lasted until 1939 when Mussolini invaded, forcing King Zog into exile. Zog's son, King Leka (1939-2011), took the oath of office as King in exile. The only living member of the Royal Family is his son, also named **Prince Leka** (b.1982). King Leka's wife, Queen Susan, died in 2004. Prince Leka is engaged to marry to Elia Zaharia

Austria:

The Habsburg family have been major players in European History since the early 1300's. In the early 1500's Holy Roman Emperor Maximilian greatly expanded his family's territories by marrying the heiress of Burgundy and marrying his children to the heirs of Hungary and Spain. From that point on, the elective office Emperor was held almost exclusively by the Habsburgs until the Empire was disbanded in 1806.

Once the Holy Roman Empire was gone, the last Emperor remained the Hereditary Emperor of Austria, King of Hungary and ruler of an extensive list of other territories in eastern and south-central Europe. Some of these lands were ceded to junior members of the family, such as Tuscany, Modena, and Teschen (southern Poland), but the core of Austria and Hungary were kept with the Emperor. The whole enchilada was lost when the Austro-German alliance lost World War I and Republicanism swept through the realms toppling all of the Germanic monarchies except the tiny Principality of Liechtenstein.

The last Emperor of Austro-Hungary was Karl I (d.1922). His eldest son and Crown Prince, Archduke Otto (1912-2011) only passed away this year. Had he been a reigning monarch, he would have the world record for longest reign at 89 years. The Head of the Imperial House is now his son and heir, **Archduke Karl** (b.1961)

Over the centuries, the Habsburg family has flourished. There are currently over 100 Archdukes of Austria and even more Archduchesses living. Some of the ones who tend to be seen at royal events in addition to those mentioned elsewhere are:

Archduke Georg (b.1964) younger son of Crown Prince Otto and married to Duchess Eilika of Oldenburg

Archduke Lorenz (b.1955) nephew of Crown Prince Otto and married to Princess Astrid of Belgium (see: Belgium)

Archduke Carl Christian (b.1954) nephew of Crown Prince Otto and married to Princess Marie-Astrid of Luxembourg (see: Luxembourg)

Archduke Simeon (b.1958) nephew of Crown Prince Otto and married to Princess Maria of the Two Sicilies. They are regular guests at Spanish royal events.

Archduke Joseph Arpád (b.1933) Head of the Hungarian branch of the family. Three generations of his direct male ancestors, ending with his grandfather, all named Joseph, served as the Imperial Governors, called Palatines, of Hungary.

Archduke Géza (b.1940) Younger brother of Joseph. He is an expert in the jewels and other priceless artifacts collected by the Imperial Family over the centuries. Lives in New York and has written several books on the subject.

Archduke Michael (b.1942) Youngest brother of Joseph. Tends to represent the family at a lot of major royal events.

Archduke Sigismondo (b.1966) *de jure* Grand Duke of Tuscany. The Habsburgs obtained Tuscany by marrying the heiress to the Medici Grand Ducal House. Emperor Leopold II ceded the Grand Duchy to his younger son, Archduke Ferdinand (Grand Duke Ferdinando III). Sigismondo is his direct descendant and heir.

Brazil:

Although in South America and not Europe, the Brazilian Imperial Family is a branch of the Portuguese Royal Family, and now, via a female inheritance, also a branch of the French Royal Family.

Emperor Pedro II (d.1891) left no male heirs, so his daughter became Head of the House that had already been removed from the

Throne. She married Prince François of Orleans of the French Royal Family, so their descendants are part of both houses.

The Headship of the house now lies with **Prince Luíz Gastão** (b. 1938) who never married. The eventual heir is his brother, **Prince Antônio** (b.1950) who is married to a granddaughter of Grand Duchess Charlotte of Luxembourg. The family has known recent tragedy as Antônio's son, Prince Pedro Luíz, was among the passengers killed in the crash of Air France flight 447 in 2009 off the coast of Brazil.

The family used to be regular guests at Spanish royal events as they were maternally cousins with King Juan Carlos's mother. However, now that generation is all gone, so there is less interaction between the families.

Bulgaria:

A somewhat more recent Monarchy, they elected as their first King a Prince from an old house: Prince Ferdinand of Saxe-Coburg and Gotha (abdicated in 1918 and d.1948). He was succeeded by his son, King Boris, who was in turn succeeded by his son, **King Simeon** (b.1937). The young King was forced into exile at the age of 9, eventually taking refuge in Spain.

Simeon came back to power in Bulgaria, not as their King, but as an elected Prime Minister in 2001, serving until 2005. He married **Margarita Gómez-Acebo**, whose cousin was married to the sister of King Juan Carlos of Spain. They have five children: **Prince Kardam** (b.1962) was in a horrific car accident in 2008 and after some improvement over time, fell back into a coma in Jan. 2010 and remains in a comatose state; **Prince Kirill** (b.1964) is a common sight at many royal events; **Prince Kubrat** (b.1965), **Prince Konstantin-Assan** (b.1967), and **Princess Kalina** (b.1972) remain mostly in private lives. All of the King's children have married and have had children of their own, bringing the number of his grandchildren to 11 to date.

The King also has a sister, **Princess Marie Louise** (b.1933) who lives in the United States and mostly stays out of the limelight.

France:

France has two royal families and each of them are involved in a dispute over who is the Head of the House.

Kingdom of France:

There has not been a French King since 1848, but this does stop the Bourbon and Orleans branches of the family from arguing over who is the *de jure* King. The argument comes down to the interpretation of the Treaty of Utrecht of 1713 which ended the War of Spanish Succession. Essentially the Treaty gave the Throne of Spain to the Bourbons but would not allow the Spanish and French Kingdoms to come under the same Crown. So King Louis XIV's grandson, the 2nd son of the Dauphin (heir to the French Throne), was chosen to become King of Spain as Felipe V. France continued to follow normal succession with some interruptions by the French Revolution and the Napoleonic French Empire until 1830 when the Bourbons were finally forced from the Throne. The male line of this branch of the family became extinct in 1885.

By 1885, the Bourbons who ruled Spain had continued but had the Throne pass through a female, Queen Isabella II, separating the Spanish Throne from the senior-most Spanish male line, which became the Carlist line in Spain. The Borbonists argue that since the senior most Spanish line was no longer the line sitting on the Spanish Throne it was okay for them to succeed to the French Throne. The snag comes when one considers that King Felipe V, upon coming to the Spanish Throne had renounced the succession to the French Throne for himself and his descendants.

Meanwhile, back in France, the French government offered the Crown to the junior most line of the Royal Family, the Orleans. The Duke of Orleans accepted and ruled as King of the French until he too was booted by a revolt in 1848. His descendants continue to argue they are the rightful Kings of France since they descend from the most recent King, and in keeping with Felipe V of Spain's renunciation.

Returning now to the 21st century, the Borbonist claim is currently in the hands of **Don Louis Alfonso de Bourbon** (b.1974) who claims the title Duke of Anjou and is regarded by his supporters as *de jure* King Louis XX. He is married to Maria Margarita Vargas and they have three children: **Eugenia** (b.2007) and twin sons, **Luis** (styled Duke of Burgundy by his father) and **Alfonso** (styled Duke of Berry) (b.2010)

The Orleanist claim is held by **Prince Henri of Orleans, Count de Paris** (b.1933). His first wife is the sister of the current claimant to the Kingdom of Württemberg, and they had five children: **Princess Marie Isabelle** (b.1959), **Prince François** (b.1961 - removed from the succession due to mental deficiency), **Princess Blanche** (b.1962), **Prince Jean** (b.1965 - styled Duke of Vendôme), and **Prince Eudes** (b.1968 - styled Duke of Angoulême).

Don Luis Alfonso is a great-grandson of King Alfonso XIII of Spain and therefore participates in several of the major Spanish royal events and the occasional French event that directly involved the old royal family. The Orleans family tend to remain in France and participate is many French cultural events. The family is quite large as the Count de Paris is one of eleven children. They do sometimes send members to the wedding of other former royals.

French Empire:
The family squabble among the Bonaparte heirs is much more recent and is between a father and a son. The titles of the former Imperial House have changed over the years, but they are reasonably uniform now that the family has dwindled to one set of siblings and their children. Members of the family are styled Prince or Princess Napoléon with the predicate Imperial Highness. The Head of the House is styled as The Prince Napoléon.

The current dispute began with the death of the most recent Prince Napoléon, Prince Louis, in 1997. In his will he disinherited his elder son and presumed heir, **Prince Charles** (b.1950), instead turning over the Headship of the House to Charles' son, **Prince Jean-Christophe** (b.1986). Charles' position is that his father did not have the authority to alter the succession by picking his own successor.

Father and son have tried to maintain a civil relationship despite the succession dispute. Most authorities in this matter side with Jean-Christophe.

Prince Charles Napoléon has been in the news the past decade for his political involvements, including running for local offices in Ajaccio and Nemours. The other members of this family are the elderly **Dowager Princess Napoléon** (b.1926 - Charles's mother), Charles' daughters: **Princess Caroline** (b.1980) and **Princess Sophie** (b.1992) and Charles' siblings: **Princess Catherine** (b.1950), **Princess Laure** (b.1952), and **Prince Jérôme** (b.1957). On the whole they do not participate much in major royal events. They do show up occasionally at Paris-based fund raisers.

Germany:

The German Empire ruled over a confederation of several German Sovereign States including the Kingdoms of Prussia (who were also the German Emperors), Württemberg, Saxony, and Bavaria, The Grand Duchies of Oldenburg, Mecklenburg, Saxe-Weimar, Baden, and Hesse and By Rhine, the Duchies of Saxe-Meiningen, Saxe-Altenburg, Saxe-Coburg, Schleswig-Holstein, Anhalt, Brunswick, the Landgravinate of Hesse, and the Principalities of Hohenzollern, Lippe, Schaumburg-Lippe, Reuss, and Waldeck.

For the most part, these families have begun to fade into obscurity. But below are some highlights of the former Kingdoms within the Empire.

Prussia:
The Royal House of Prussia came to rule over the rest of Germany with the formation of the German Empire in 1871. There were three Emperor (or Kaisers): Wilhelm I, Frederick III, and Wilhelm II. The Empire and all of its royal and princely subcomponents were swept away by Revolution in the ending days of World War I in November 1918.

The Prussian Royal Family is now headed up by **Prince Georg Friedrich** (b.1976). He has several cousins, but they have mostly become private citizens with daily jobs and generally only show up for royal event that take place within their own family. Prince Georg Friedrich married Princess Sophie of Isenburg, in Aug 2011, momentarily shining modern press light on this ancient house.

Bavaria:
Like all German states, Bavaria has not had a King since 1918, but someone has forgotten to tell the Bavarians. The treat their royal family now much like they did before the Wars. The current head of the family is **Franz, Duke of Bavaria** (b.1933). As he has never married, his heir is his brother, **Prince Max**. Max holds two Bavarian titles. He was adopted by the last of a distant non-reigning branch of the family who were titled Dukes in Bavaria, so he bears this title as well as Prince of Bavaria, which denotes he is from the former reigning line. The eldest of Max's five daughters, **Princess Sophie** is now the Hereditary Princess of Liechtenstein (see: Liechtenstein).

Several members of the elder generation, that now is all but gone, married into other reigning families so there are close genealogical ties between the Bavarians, the Habsburgs, the Bourbons of Sicily and Spain, and the Brazilians. This means one can expect Bavarian representation at the weddings and funerals of most of these families.

Saxony:
The Royal Family of Saxony has dwindled greatly since its heyday. The current claimant to the long vacancy Throne is **Maria Emanuel, Margrave of Meissen** (b.1926). With no other eligible males left in his family, he decreed that his heir shall be his sister's son **Prince Alexander** (b.1954) who took the Saxony title and is married to **Princess Gisela of Bavaria**. The couple has four children, three of whom are boys so the family should continue now.

Like many of the German royals, they really do not participate much in events that do not directly involve their family.

Württemberg
Over the past two hundred years, this family has provided many
royal brides. But the male lines, which were very numerous in
1850 are now down to one.

The Head of the Family is **Karl, Duke of Württemberg** (b.1936).
He is married to **Princess Diane of France**, sister of the Orleanist
claimant to the French Throne. Their six children, four of whom
are boys, are doing their part to repopulate this family.

The Duke and his wife do tend to participate in royal events more
than most Germany families, but that is mostly due to the large
number of inter-relationships with the Duchess's large family.

Greece:
The Greek Royal Family is a branch of the Danish Royal Family.
When Greece was looking to elect a new King, they selected
Prince George of Denmark, King Christian IX's second son.

Never a stable Throne, the final expulsion of the Royal Family
from Greece happened in 1967. The monarchy was finally
abolished in 1973.

Today, the Greek Royal Family is limited to **King Constantine II**,
his wife, the former Princess Anne-Marie of Denmark (see:
Denmark for more details) their children and grandchildren and a
2nd cousin, **Prince Michael** (b.1939) and his daughters **Princess
Alexandra** (b.1968) and **Princess Olga** (b.1971)

King Constantine and his immediate family are regular guests at
most royal events throughout Europe.

Italy:
The Kingdom of Italy existed from 1861 until 1946. Before that
the Italian peninsula was made up of a series of smaller states, the
ones with families left to be discussed are the Kingdom of
Sardinia, which is the family (Savoy) that unified Italy, the

Kingdom of the Two Sicilies, The Grand Duchy of Tuscany (see: Austria), and the Duchy of Parma.

House of Savoy
This long standing family has been a major force in Franco-Italian affairs for centuries. They had been Counts and then Dukes of Savoy in southeastern France since the beginning of the 11th century. By 1720, they had gained enough territory to form the Kingdom of Sardinia. But they did not stop there, they went for the whole of Italy, finally unifying all of the peninsula into one Kingdom in 1861. The Kingdom did not withstand World War II and fell to the desires of Republicanism in 1946.

Like so many royal families now, there are only a few members of the family left. In this family's case, it is because they had innumerable daughters but very few sons. For example, the last King, Umberto II, was the only boy out of a family of five children. The current head of the House is his son, himself the only boy out of four children, **Prince Vittorio Emanuele, The Prince of Naples** (b. 1937). He has an only child, **Prince Emanuele Filiberto** (b.1972) who is the father of two small daughters, so far.

Unless more males are born to this senior line, the Headship of the House will pass to the branch of the Dukes of Aosta, headed up by the current Duke, **Prince Amedeo** (b.1943). He has a son, **Prince Aimone** (b.1967) who is married to Princess Olga of Greece and has a son, **Prince Umberto** (b.2009)

Prince Emanuele Filiberto and his wife sometimes attend royal events, but there have been several recent scandals within his family which has lead them to maintain a low profile.

The Kingdom of the Two Sicilies:
This is actually a branch of the Royal House of Spain as King Carlos III ceded Naples and Sicily to his younger son, Ferdinand. Ferdinand changed the name to the Two Sicilies as their were two areas both claiming the title Kingdom of Sicily. With them now united under one Crown, this was the title that was chosen.

By the early 1800's there were numerous branches of the Sicilian Royal Family starting to blossom. There were also numerous Princesses of this House. This lead to all major Catholic Royal Families to become very closely related through these princesses.

The Two Sicilies ceased being an independent country when it was annexed by Sardinia to form the unified Italy. The last King to reign was Francesco II (d.1894). Francesco, having no surviving children, was succeeded by his brother, Alfonso, Count of Caserta (d.1934) and he by his son, Ferdinand (d.1960) and here is where another succession argument comes about.

Sicily only allowed male succession, so while Ferdinand had 3 surviving children they were all daughters and could not succeed. His next younger brother, Carlos, had married the heir to the Spanish Throne, but she never succeeded. In order to marry her, Carlos was obliged to renounce his succession rights in Sicily which he did for himself and his descendants. When Ferdinand died in 1960, Carlos's son Alfonso, claimed his father's renunciation was void because his wife never inherited Spain and now there was a different line on that Throne.

Meanwhile, Carlos's next younger brother, Rainieri, was saying that a renunciation is a renunciation and that he was the rightful heir to the Two Sicilies.

This dispute continues today between the descendants of Carlos and Rainieri. On the Carlos line, the Family is headed up by **Infante Carlos of Spain, Duke of Calabria** (b.1938) a first cousin to the King of Spain. He is married to Princess Anne of France, a sister of the Orleanist claimant to the French Throne. They have five children, only one of whom is a boy, **Prince Pedro** who married unequally and his children are barred from succeeding. So it appears this lines claim is due to die out.

On the line descended from Prince Rainieri, the head is **Prince Charles**, who also uses the title **Duke of Calabria** (b.1963). His marriage is not recognized as equal by the Carlos branch, but was recognized by his father, who was at the time also claiming to be

118

Head of the House. But again, we may be headed for a moot point as Charles only has two daughters.

So assuming there is no change in the status quo, both the Carlos and Rainieri lines will die out and the Claim will pass to the descendants of the youngest line, that of Prince Gabriel (d.1975) whose eldest son, **Antoine** (b.1929) married a Duchess of Württemberg and their eldest son, **Francesco** (b.1960) is married to a Countess of Schönborn, who is of unquestionable equality.

Infante Carlos, and his family generally participate in Spanish royal events. **Prince Charles** and his sister, **Princess Beatrice** can often been seen at royal events taking place in France.

Parma
They Duchy of Parma is another branch of the Spanish Royal Family. King Felipe V married the heiress of the Farnese Dukes of Parma receiving the Duchy in the process. He then ceded it to his youngest surviving son, who became Duke Filippo. The family remained rather compact until the last reigning Duke, Roberto I, came along and fathered 24 children.

After spending some time in the senior line before it became extinct, the Headship of the house fell to Sisto, one of Roberto's younger sons. He died in 1977 and was succeeded by his son, Carlos Hugo who was married to the sister of Queen Beatrix of the Netherlands. He died in 2010, and the current Duke is his elder son **Prince Carlos Javier** (b.1970). The new Duke was scheduled to get married about the time his father died, so the wedding was delayed a few months. Until he has a son, his heir is his brother, **Prince Jaime** (b.1972). However, the Duke and Duchess have announced they expect their first child in May, 2012. The immediate family of the Duke is often seen at Dutch royal events. (see: Netherlands).

There are junior branches to the Bourbon-Parma family. They include the Grand Ducal House of Luxembourg since Duke Sisto's next younger brother, Felix, married Grand Duchess Charlotte.

However, in 1987, The Grand Duke of Luxembourg renounced all Bourbon-Parma titles and succession rights.

Next is the line descended from the next brother, Prince René. He married Princess Margrethe of Denmark. This branch has mostly remained in Denmark and stays out of the public eye.

The last line is descended from Prince Louis, next to youngest of Duke Robert's 24 children. He married Princess Maria, one of the sisters of King Umberto II of Italy. Their descendants also maintain a low profile, but in France.

Montenegro:
Montenegro had been ruled by the house of Petrovic-Njegos since 1696, mostly as reigning princes until 1910 when Prince Nikola I declared he was King. Eight years later Montenegro was annexed into Serbia and eventually formed into the Kingdom of Yugoslavia. Montenegro has re-established itself as a independent state since 2006, but as a Republic.

Nikola was succeed by his son, Danilo (III) who abdicated his Throne in exile a short time later. Danilo was succeeded by his nephew, Michael, who died in 1986. Since then the head of the House has been Michael's son, **Nikola** (III) (b.1944).

The Montenegrin Royal Family is very small, being made up by the current claimant, his daughter **Princess Altinai** (b.1977) and his son and heir, **Prince Boris** (b.1980). Boris married in 2007 and so far has only a daughter, **Princess Milena** (b.2008). As there are no other branches surviving of the family, it will become extinct if Boris does not produce a male heir.

The Montenegrin Royal Family does not participate in public events.

Portugal:
Portugal had been ruled by the Bragança family in the 1600's. The monarchy came to an end in 1910 when a Republic was established.

The Portuguese Royal Family today is limited to the present head, **Duarte, Duke of Bragança** (b.1945), his wife, Isabel, his children: **Dom Afonso** (b.1996), **Dona Maria Francisca** (b.1997) and **Dom Dinis** (b.1991), and the Duke's two unmarried brothers, **Dom Miguel** (b.1946) and **Dom Henrique** (b.1949). All of these family members are styled Infante or Infanta of Portugal with the predicate Royal Highness.

The Duke and Duchess of Bragança are regular guests at most major royal events.

Romania:
The Kingdom of Romania was established in 1881 with Prince Karl of Hohenzollern on the Throne as King Carol I. He was succeeded by his nephew, King Ferdinand whose wife was the quixotic Queen Marie, born a British princess and granddaughter of Queen Victoria.

Ferdinand and Marie's elder son was a bit of a problem King. While he was still Crown Prince, he abandoned his military post to elope with his girlfriend, Zizi Lambrino. The marriage was invalidated, but Carol and Zizi still had a son who took the name Carol when he got older.

Carol later entered into a more appropriate, albeit extremely unhappy, marriage with Princess Helen of Greece. The marriage eventually ended in divorce but not before Helen had the needed son and heir, Michael.

King Michael (b.1921), after his father abdicated in 1940, only got to reign or seven years before he was forced out by the Communists. Michael married **Princess Anne of Bourbon-Parma** and they have five daughters: **Princess Margarita** (b.1949), **Princess Helen** (b.1950), **Princess Irina** (b.1953) **Princess Sophie** (b.1957), and **Princess Maria** (b.1964)

Michael has re-established a residence in Romania and has been restored some of the Royal Family's property. With no male heirs,

King Michael has decreed that his heiress is his eldest daughter and that she will be followed by the son of his 2nd daughter (Margarita has no children), now **Prince Nicholas** (b.1985)

King Michael has been a regular guest at all major royal events, including the 2011 marriage of the Duke of Cambridge. But as his age progresses, he is delegating more and more duties to his daughter and heiress, Crown Princess Margarita and her husband, Prince Radu

The illegitimate son of Zizi Lambrino, Carol, took the name Hohenzollern in 1955 and died in 2006. He left two sons by different wives, Paul and Alexander. The younger has no significant contact with any of his father's family. The elder has led a campaign to be acknowledged as a Prince of Romania, a title to which he has no legitimate claim. However, the Romanian authorities tolerate him and allowed him to change his name to **Paul al Romanai** which is Romanian for "Paul of Romania". He married in 1996 a woman approaching 50, but yet, with substantial medical assistance, managed to produce a son, named Carol in 2010.

Russia:

The Romanov Family came to power in Russia when Michael Romanov was elected Tsar in 1613. A century later, his descendant, Peter the Great, would westernize the country and his own title to Emperor of Russia. Peter's descendants would sit on the Throne until it is swept away by the Bolshevik Revolution in 1918. The Bolsheviks attempted to kill as many members of the Imperial Family as they could, but several did escape.

The current headship of the Imperial House is somewhat disputed but most authorities now recognize **Grand Duchess Maria** (b.1953) has the Head of the House. Her own opinion of the situation is that the Imperial House has only two members at the moment, herself and her son, **Grand Duke George** (b.1981).

Whether they are legitimately entitled to the Headship of the House depends on if the marriage of Maria's parents, Grand Duke

Wladimir and Princess Leonida Bagration was considered equal or not. Most of the other male-line Romanoffs (now using the westernized spelling) do not believe it is. They argue Leonida was no more or less equal than several of their own mothers, yet they were considered unequal and therefore their children would have no succession rights.

Even expanding the equality definition to include the other living male lines, the numbers are quickly dwindling. The next line to Maria in that of the Princes Ilyinsky, descended from Alexander II's youngest legitimate son. This line only has two males, **Prince Dmitry** (b.1954) and **Prince Michael** (b.1959), after them, we go to the descendants of Nicholas I's third son, Grand Duke Nicholas. This line also only has two males, and elderly ones at that: **Prince Nicolas** (b.1922) and his brother, **Prince Dmitry** (b.1926)

After them, the remaining lines are descended from Grand Duke Alexander and his wife, who was Emperor Nicholas II's sister, Xenia. The eldest of these is **Prince Andrew** (b.1923) who has three middle-aged sons, and an only granddaughter. The next living males are the sons of Prince Rostislav (d.1999): **Rostislav** (b.1985) and **Nikita** (b.1987). Their first cousins live in America and have been raised totally away from the Romanov family and its traditions, but there is a hope of keeping the male line alive there: **Nick Romanoff** (b.1968) has two young daughters, so a son is still possible. His brother, **Daniel Romanoff** (b.1972) has recently given the family hope with son **Jackson** (b.2009).

None of the male Romanoffs participate in any royal events unless they relate directly to the Romanov family. However, Grand Duchess Maria has recently stepped up her visibility and that of her son at major events. George is to the age he needs to be finding a wife, but has a limited pool to select from since he must marry equally.

Yugoslavia:
The Kingdom of Yugoslavia was created by combining the principalities of Serbia, Croatia, and Slovenia in 1929 under King

Alexander I. It only lasted until 1945 when King Peter II was forced into exile and the monarchy abolished.

After the fall of the Communists and the Milosevic regime, Yugoslavia was taken back apart into it original components. The Royal Family has remained with Serbia, now calling themselves Princes and Princesses of Serbia.

The family is headed up by **Crown Prince Alexander** (b.1945) the only child of the last King. His first wife, and the mother of his children, is Princess Maria da Gloria of the House of Brazil. They are divorced and he married his second wife, **Katharine**, in 1985. His children by the first marriage, **Princes Peter** (b.1980) and twins **Philip** and **Alexander** (b.1982) make up the core of the family. There are some cousins still around, but it is this core that generally represents the family at royal events. Crown Prince Alexander and his wife are frequent invitees and guests to all major royal events.

One cousin, **Princess Elizabeth** is better know to Americans as the mother of actress Catherine Oxenberg.

In Memoriam

Those members of the reigning and formerly reigning families who died in 2011:

12 Jan: **H.I.&R.H. Duchess Ilona of Mecklenburg** (b.1927) née Archduchess of Austria, sister of Archduke Joseph, head of the Hungarian branch of the family. Her former husband was Duke Georg Alexander of Mecklenburg, who was head of the Grand Ducal House of Mecklenburg-Strelitz

4 Feb: **H.H. Duchess Gertrude of Oldenburg** (b.1926) née Princess of Löwenstein-Wertheim-Freudenberg, wife of Duke Peter of Oldenburg, one of several grandsons of the last Grand Duke.

11 Mar: **Jörg Brena** (b.1921) (né **H.H. Prince of Saxe-Weimar-Eisenach**) grandson of the last Grand Duke of Saxony, he was one of only a few male members of the family left.

18 Mar: **H.S.H. Princess Antoinette of Monaco** (b.1920) sister of Sovereign Prince Rainier III, and aunt of current Sovereign Prince Albert II.

18 Apr: **H.R.H. Princess Thereza of Orleans and Bragança** (b.1919) granddaughter of the last Princess Imperial of Brazil. She was the widow of commoner Ernesto Martorell

6 May: **H.S.H. Princess Laura of Liechtenstein** (b.1941) né Campeggi. She was the wife of Prince Franz, a distant cousin to the Sovereign Prince.

13 May: **H.I.&R.H. Princess Maria of Orleans and Bragança** (b.1914) né Princess of Bavaria. The de jure Dowager Empress. Her husband, Prince Pedro Henrique, was Head of the Imperial House 1921-1981.

4 Jul: **H.I.&R.H. Archduke Otto, Crown Prince of Austria, etc.** (b.1912) Son of Emperor Karl, he was the last of the World War I

era crown princes. He served as Head of the Imperial House for 89 years, a world record.

8 Jul: H.I.&R.H. Archduchess Marie Valerie of Austria (b.1913) née Countess von Waldburg-Zeil-Hohenems. Her husband, Archduke Georg, was a grandson of the last Grand Duke of Tuscany.

13 Jul: H.R.H. Princess Katrin of Saxe-Coburg and Gotha (b.1940) né Bremme. The de jure Dowager Duchess. Her husband, Prince Friedrich Josias, was Head of the Ducal House 1972-1998.

18 Aug: Maria Theresia Desewffy de Csernek et Tarkö (b.1953) née Princess of Liechtenstein. A great-niece of Sovereign Prince Franz-Josef II, father of the current Sovereign Prince.

7 Sep: H.I.&R.H. Archduke Felix of Austria (b.1916) a younger son of the last Emperor of Austria.

12 Sep: H.R.H. Prince Rasso of Bavaria (b.1926) a grandson of the last King of Bavaria.

22 Sep: H.S.H. The Baroness Grand d'Esnon (b.1924) née Princess Reuss. The Principality of Reuss is best known for the fact that all of its men are named Heinrich. They use an elaborate numbering system to denote eeach Prince Heinrich. She was a daughter of the last Sovereign Prince, Heinrich XXXIX.

Oct: H.R.H. Prince André of Bourbon-Parma (b.1928) grandson of the last reigning Duke of Parma. His mother was Princess Margarethe of Denmark, a granddaugher of King Christian IX.

13 Oct: Countess Henriette von und zu Eltz (b.1914) née Princess of Liechtenstein, she was an aunt of the current Sovereign Prince, and the last surviving sibling of Prince Franz Josef II. She was the widow of Count Peter von und zu Eltz who died in 1992.

24 Oct: **H.I.&R.H. Archduke István of Austria** (b.1934) brother of Archduke Joseph, head of the Hungarian Branch. His sister, Ilona died eariler in the year.

24 Oct: **The Marquesa de Beniel** (b.1960) Ana Isabel de Borbón was a direct male-line descendant of Infante Enrique of Spain, Duke of Seville (1823-1870) who was a grandson of King Carlos IV.

19 Nov: **H.S.H. Princess Angelica Ilyinsky** (b.1932) née Angelica Kauffmann. She was the daughter-in-law of Grand Dmitri of Russia, one of the co-conspirators in the murder of Rasputin. Her late husband, Prince Paul, was the senior male representative of Tsar Peter III (husband of Catherine the Great) who had been Duke of Holstein-Gottorp before becoming Tsar. Grand Duke Dmitri's marriage was considered unequal under Russian succession rules, but not under Holstein's. So, Angelica was the de jure Dowager Duchess of Holstein-Gottop.

22 Nov: **H.H. The Dowager Duchess of Hohenberg** (b.1922) née Princess Elisabeth of Luxembourg. She was a sister of Grand Duke Jean of Luxembourg and an aunt of the current Grasnd Duke. Her late husband, Duke Franz Ferdinand, was a grandson of Archduke Franz Ferdinand of Austria, whose murder sparked World War I.

21 Nov: **H.H. Princess Christina of Hesse** (b.1933) was a niece of Britain's Duke of Edinburgh and was once married to Prince Andrej of Yugoslavia, brother of the last King.

30 Nov: **H.M. King Leka of the Albanians** (b.1939) never reigned as King, but was proclaimed King while exile. Later in life he was afforded a degree of recognition by the Albania government. His funeral was conducted as for a former Head of State.

14614216R00068

Made in the USA
Lexington, KY
09 April 2012